Kissing an Old Dream Goodbye

A MEMOIR
1950 – 1959

Gloria Levi

FICTIVE
PRESS

A **FICTIVE PRESS** Book

First published in 2019 by Fictive Press, a division of BizNet Communications (2815699 Canada Inc.), British Columbia, Canada.
fictivepress.com

Some names and particulars have been changed to protect the privacy of individuals.

"An Arab Shepherd is Searching for his Goat on Mount Zion" by Yehuda Amichai, with permission from Sheep Meadow Press.

Front cover photo and back cover background photo, provided by Gloria Levi: Stone cottage at Kfar Daniel, Israel, 1957
Back cover photo, provided by Gloria Levi: Gloria Levi and Norman Levi, Toronto, 1951
Author photo by Susan Curtis
Cover design by Fictive Press

Library and Archives Canada Cataloguing in Publication
Title: Kissing an old dream goodbye : a memoir, 1950-1959 / Gloria Levi.
Names: Levi, Gloria, author.
Identifiers: Canadiana (print) 20189069066 |
Canadiana (ebook) 20189069074 |
ISBN 9781927663677 (softcover) | ISBN 9781927663684 (Kindle) |
ISBN 9781927663691 (EPUB)
Subjects: LCSH: Levi, Gloria. | LCSH: Jews, American—Israel—
Biography. | LCSH: Jews, Canadian—Israel—Biography. | LCSH: Israel—
Biography. |
LCGFT: Autobiographies.
Classification: LCC DS113.8.A4 L48 2019 |
DDC 956.94/004924073092—dc23

Kissing an Old Dream Goodbye

Praise for *Kissing an Old Dream Goodbye*

"A riveting read from beginning to end. The story of a remarkable woman whose life intersected with a critical time in Jewish history. Levi captures the struggles of a young woman striving for personal identity and family balance, with the backdrop of a similarly young country striving to find its identity. She writes with insight, humour, honesty and passion, in a book you won't be able to put down." — Mark L. Winston is a Professor and Senior Fellow at Simon Fraser University's Morris J. Wosk Centre for Dialogue, and author of the 2015 Governor General's Nonfiction Literary Award for Bee Time: Lessons From the Hive.

"In contrast to the better known narratives of the refugee Aliya and the Middle East in the first decade of the State of Israel, this is the seldom told story of a young Anglo family, impelled to immigrate to the newly born state by Zionist idealism, hope and a sense of adventure. The exhilaration of realizing their dream is soon mixed with the pettiness, doubt and drudgery of daily life in the new state, followed by their heartbreaking resignation. A captivating personal story in all its detail and complexity." — Rahel Halabe is an eminent Arabic/Hebrew translator in Israel, a gifted Hebrew teacher and author of the two volume innovative textbook, *Hinei, an Introduction to Biblical Hebrew*.

"A heartfelt journey where young idealism encounters the real struggles of young immigrants to the newly formed State of Israel. Levi's experience as a pioneer in Israel during those early years foreshadowed the complex challenges that would grow for the young country as it became more established. She leaves the reader smelling and feeling the land of Israel from the 1950s, with all its brilliance and troubles." — Rabbi Yonatan Gordis is a partner at ChangeCraft, a consulting firm specializing in change processes in the philanthropic and non-profit fields, and a director of *Sh'ma Now*.

To my grandmother, Basha Riva,
who lived in Jewish time and embodied
the character traits (midot) of compassion and love.
She taught me the beauty and wonder of Jewish ritual.

Contents

CHAPTER 1

Stars in My Eyes

Im tirtsu, ain zu agada.
If you will it, it is no dream.
— Theodore Herzl

Standing on the Marseilles pier, Norman told me later, he noticed me immediately. I was a short, slender young woman with shoulder-length, wavy brown hair. I wore a long tweedy-brown raincoat, paint box in hand, guitar strung over my shoulder. I neither painted nor played the guitar. Norman saw me as some kind of bohemian. I stood in line as I waited to board the SS Negba, an Israeli ship taking hundreds of Moroccan Jews from Marseilles to settle in the new State of Israel. Old men with their Torahs, women in their colourful kaftans, and hundreds of children, many with shaved heads, who had been treated for ringworm or eye disease. I was 19 years old, impatient to set sail for Israel, the land of my dreams.

I spent my teen years in the Labour Zionist movement and dreamed of becoming a pioneer in Israel. I had read many of the earlier Labour Zionist ideologues,

Jewish history and socialist writers. I grew up in Brooklyn, New York. Emotionally, socially and culturally, I was surrounded by Jews and rarely met non-Jews. I was fiercely independent and a bit of a rebel, and had a stormy relationship with my mother. My father had died when I was eleven. I paid my own way through university and had recently been living independently in Greenwich Village.

I had just completed my first year at New York University, majoring in psychology and philosophy. However, I began to intellectually question and doubt many of my basic assumptions. This summer trip would be an opportunity to test my values and ideals. Could I live as an American and a Jew? What did I really want out of life? Who did I want to become? What did "self-realization" really mean?

As I headed to my cabin, I was startled to find a middle-aged man there. He was speaking German to his wife. Not knowing how to handle the situation, I turned to the young man in the neighboring cabin and said, "There's a man in my cabin!" On this, the lowest deck, there was a hold for the dozens of children, and two cabins, one designated for women and one for men. The young man, who introduced himself as Norman, promptly entered my cabin, spoke to the man in German and arranged for him to share his cabin as intended.

Norman was of medium height, with broad shoulders and a strong muscular torso. He wore large thick glasses that hid his warm, large blue-green eyes. He

2

had high cheekbones, a square firm chin, wavy brown hair. I was immediately attracted to him and to his beautifully deep resonant voice and British accent. And, clearly the feelings were mutual.

Norman had joined the British Army's tank corps in 1944 and was in Germany as the war ended. He had been with the British troops who liberated Buchenwald concentration camp. In 1947, he was deployed to India during the bloody time of Partition. When he was demobilized, Norman had difficulty adjusting to civilian life. He was restless. When Israel declared its independence and the five surrounding Arab nations attacked the country, Norman volunteered and fought with the *Machal* (overseas volunteers). Having experienced many life-and-death situations, Norman was an emotionally mature 23-year-old, returning to settle in Israel.

It was 1950, two years after the Declaration of Independence of the new State of Israel. The ship landed at the Haifa harbour and passengers began to disembark. Bearded old Moroccan Jewish men, tears streaming down their faces as they carried a Torah scroll in their arms, marched down the gangplank and bent to kiss the ground of the Holy Land. From the upper deck, I watched with tears in my eyes and felt the poignancy of the moment. It was like a scene in a Hollywood movie, only this was real life.

I had arranged to visit friends from the Habonim movement at Kibbutz Gesher Haziv. Norman had army buddies at Moshav Habonim and joined them. However, ignoring our newfound romance was intolerable to me. So, after three days at Gesher Haziv, I said goodbye to my friends, put my rucksack on my back and hitchhiked to Moshav Habonim. Norman and I made our base on this South African modified kibbutz, a *meshek shitufi*, a cooperative settlement south of Haifa. Life on Moshav Habonim reaffirmed my expectations. It was a *chevra* (social group) of young singles and couples. They were welcoming, hard working and dedicated to the building of a new nation.

Norman worked with a team on the beach, sieving vermiculite, a product used for insulation. It was hot tiring work and highly respected. I worked mainly in the services, in the kitchen, dining area or laundry. When I objected as a women's rights supporter, they gave me a demeaning job in the metal workshop — straightening nails! I finally gave up, realizing I could not buck the subtle male chauvinism even in a so-called egalitarian place.

Nevertheless, I was a people person and found communal living endlessly challenging and fascinating. Life was idyllic. I was in love. I was helping in the building of the new State of Israel. I was surrounded by young idealistic, inspired people.

I arranged to meet some of my Israeli relatives, Mordechai and Chana Siletsky. They were thrilled to meet me and welcomed me and Norman warmly. They had come from Pennsylvania, where Mordechai had worked as a shoe salesman. They had eight daughters: Ahoova, Shoshana, Sara, Metukah, Drora, Dvorah, and twin babies, Yehudit and Chaya. In Pennsylvania, Shoshana, at 15, had begun dating a boy who was not Jewish. Mordechai, an ardent Zionist and concerned about his daughters' interfaith choices and their futures, decided to immigrate to Palestine.

In 1923, Mordechai joined a *moshav ovdim*, a cooperative farming village in Balfouria near Afula. He owned 10 *dunam*, about two and a half acres. All the buying and selling in the village was done cooperatively. The family had survived the draining of the swamps, malaria, illness, poor crops, and hostile Arab neighbours. As a farmer, Mordechai very much wanted a son. However, when Chana gave birth to their last child, it was a girl. They named her Ruth. Nine daughters! All of them proud Zionists, devoted to family and rooted in the land. I found joy and pride in being with them.

Since Moshav Habonim was settled mostly by South Africans, little Hebrew was spoken there, so I decided to study Hebrew at an *ulpan* (language centre) near Pardes Hana. We worked four hours in the fields in the mornings and studied Hebrew all afternoon. I had only one semester of Hebrew at New York University in which the emphasis was on reading and grammar. The *ulpan* focused mainly on conversation. I discovered that I had a good ear for languages. Norman and I frequently met on weekends.

There were 17 students on the *ulpan*, the majority from Iraq. Our only common language was Hebrew. Many of the Iraqis were highly educated professionals: pharmacists, teachers, accountants, etc. They took me under their wing. I thoroughly enjoyed their company and developed a deep respect for Iraqi-Jewish culture.

Close to Pardes Hana was a large *ma'abara* (transition camp) consisting mainly of tin huts. Seeing men behind wire fences, dressed in what looked like pajamas, seemed very strange to me. I asked Sara, my Hebrew teacher, for an explanation.

"The Jewish population in Israel has nearly doubled," she said. "It grew from just over 600,000 in 1948 to 1,150,000. Eighty per cent of the new immigrants have come or been expelled from Arab or Muslim countries — Yemen, Iraq, Libya. We're building new housing as fast as possible. But it is impossible to keep up with such a demand."

"I've been reading about the speed and determination of the State to build new housing. But I had never put it together with the *ma'abarot.*"

"We will continue to take in Jews from everywhere. Forget the stereotype. There is no one Jewish face. We are a polyglot people united by only one thing — The Book. That is what we have in common: Torah. We are building a Jewish state. This is our dream. This is my dream."

"I think this is my dream too, Sara. I love this land."

Norman and two of his buddies were not ready to make a long-term commitment to Moshav Habonim, so they decided to leave and strike out on their own. They found paid work plowing in Degania Bet, close to Lake Kinneret (Sea of Galilee). I left the *ulpan* and joined Norman there, working on the kibbutz for my room and board.

A *kvutza* is a smaller collective than a kibbutz, by design. I had read about the history of the Second Aliyah, the second wave of immigration to Israel, which took place between 1904 and 1914. Several notable ideologues of the State of Israel founded the two *kvutzot*, Degania Alef and Degania Bet. They included such luminaries as A. D. Gordon and the national poet, Rachel Bluwstein. One of the founders of Degania Bet was Levi Eshkol, Israel's third prime minister. For me, being in Degania Bet felt like stepping into the pages of history.

The highlight of my time in Degania was a concert at Ein Gev, a kibbutz on the other side of Lake Kinneret. Busloads of *kibutznikim*, farmers in their open-necked white shirts with rolled-up sleeves, poured in and filled every orange-crate seat. The terrain, shaped like an amphitheatre, rolled down toward the Sea of Galilee. It was a sight to behold. We listened raptly to the performance of Bach. The musicians were superb; the music divine; the audience enthusiastic. This event was one of those inspiring, unforgettable moments.

It was September. I did not consider whether or not to extend my time in Israel. I simply followed my heart to see where it might lead. I did not care to give myself any deadlines to return to the United States. My studies could wait.

Later that fall, Norman and his two friends decided to acquire a boat and sail around the world, with the intention of meeting up with me at some point in the United States. They arranged to meet an Arab boat builder named Ali, in Akko (Acre), to discuss the boat build. Numerous meetings and endless negotiations in Akko began.

Ali spoke no English or Hebrew so two of his friends, Mustafa and Muchmood, volunteered to act as interpreters. Muchmood had worked in the oil refinery in Haifa but was dismissed because the authorities believed that all Arabs were a security risk. Mustafa was the village blacksmith. His young wife, Subhia, was a stunning beauty, an Arab version of the Canadian actress, Geneviève Bujold. Subhia had two children, Jihad and Muchmood, and was pregnant with her third child. Her eldest child was called Jihad, Holy War, because he had been born during the Israeli War of Independence, when Mustafa, along with other Arab men of Akko, had been jailed as potential security risks.

Negotiations with Ali always took several days. It was a ritual dance. We came. We feasted in the public square adjacent to the blacksmith and boatbuilding shops. Then we talked. The meal — goat-cheese balls dipped in pure olive oil, pita, hummus mixed with *t'china* (tahini), diced tomatoes, cucumbers and green peppers — was lowered by rope from the window of Ali's home.

Hospitality is a core value of Arab culture. They told us, "If a person is within your gates, he must be treated as if he were your brother." We wandered in and out the back streets and plazas of Akko. Whenever I asked Mustafa when a square or building had been built, he would reply, "*Lifnei* Sultan Siklazj" (before the reign of Sultan Siklazj), an expression that meant "way back when."

We would often have lunch at the Abu Christo café overlooking the sea. The table would be laden with a variety of salads, hummus, falafel, lamb kebabs, and sometimes fried eggs with cinnamon, usually accompanied by the ubiquitous Arabic coffee with *hel,* cardamom seed.

Measurements were described by hand and elbow lengths. Ali built dhow-like fishing boats that hugged the shoreline and did not have a keel. They were never meant for ocean sailing. Most negotiations lasted approximately three days. Finally, Norman realized that Ali could not build a seafaring vessel.

In the course of these meetings, Norman and I developed a deep and abiding relationship with Mustafa and his family. Mustafa was a skilled artisan, a fair and honourable man, who was highly respected in his community. Subhia was attentive to the needs of the women in her community and much loved. Politics never entered into our relationship. There was nothing but genuine warmth and respect in all our dealings.

Norman and I then spent a month in the southern part of Israel, on Kibbutz Kfar Menachem, where I learned that Israelis often plowed the land without cultivating or sowing it. Under old Turkish law, ploughing the land gave a person or group a political claim to it. So, Norman was paid to do "political plowing" on this isolated southern kibbutz.

While visiting friends in Tel Aviv in December, I received a telegram from my mother, informing me that my beloved grandmother was dying. Heartbroken, I hastily made arrangements to fly home. Norman and I spoke of our commitment to each other, promising to reunite in the United States. At the airport, we kissed goodbye. With tears in my eyes, I walked past the gate, into the KLM airplane and flew home. I resumed my university studies in January, and waited patiently for Norman to join me.

CHAPTER 2

Tumultuous Beginnings

Then, welcome each rebuff
That turns earth's smoothness rough,
Each sting that bids nor sit nor stand but go! Be our joy three-parts pain!
Strive, and hold cheap the strain;
Learn, nor account the pang; dare never grudge the throe!
— Robert Browning, "Rabbi Ben Ezra"

I decided to major in child psychology and transferred to the University of Iowa in Iowa City, renowned for its child psychology department, to finish my undergraduate degree. It was a picturesque campus in the heart of the Corn Belt, with the Iowa River running through it, much green space, trees and blooming flowers. The professors and student body were challenging and intellectually stimulating. I loved it.

After numerous and frustrating attempts to realize his sailing dream, Norman gave it up and flew to England, where he worked and saved money.

Eleven months later, on American Thanksgiving, 1951, Norman and I were reunited in the main Chicago train station, which still maintained an aura of 1920s grandeur about it. We met halfway down the grand staircase of the station. It was a highly dramatic moment, right out of a romance novel. Norman had a 30-day transit visa for the United States. We traveled back to Iowa City, remaining there until his transit visa was about to expire.

"Norman, this isn't Israel. Perhaps in this new setting of North America, we should first live together and see if it works for us."

"One way or the other, I'm committed," he said firmly.

"I know, but I'm worried about university policy and my career. I think I should speak to my advisor about possible consequences."

In the 1950s, you could be expelled from university if caught "living in sin." My advisor pointed out that I would be jeopardizing my career if we lived together without being married. He said, "I grant you that if you are married and decide to split, divorce can be messy. But so can the split-up of deeply committed relationships."

I returned to Norman and shrugged. "I guess we'll just have to get married." So much for romantic proposals!

Just before my Christmas break, we decided to cross the border from Detroit to Windsor, Ontario, so Norman could get his passport stamped as a landed Canadian immigrant. In those days, British citizens had an automatic right to immigrate to Canada. We intended to travel to New Jersey to meet my family and marry there. We crossed back from Windsor to Detroit, where an unexpected confrontation with immigration authorities erupted. After a two-hour interrogation and no explanation — it was the height of the McCarthy era and paranoia was rampant — Norman was barred from entering the United States for one year. There we were, stranded in Windsor, Ontario, with limited funds and only a few weeks left before I had to return to university.

"What shall we do?" I asked Norman, totally perplexed.

Norman thought for a moment and said, "I have a friend in Toronto, Moe Schwartz. We were together in the tanks in Israel in '48. I think he might be able to help us."

We hitchhiked to Toronto and Moe invited us into the house he shared with his parents and sisters. He contacted his Orthodox rabbi and arranged for us to meet him. We rented a room in the attic of a friend of Moe's family.

On Saturday afternoon, December 22, 1951, the sky was dark and it was snowing heavily. The Toronto buses and trolleys were on strike. At three o'clock, we began trudging through the snow toward Moe's house. Forty minutes later, we arrived, tired, wet, and chilled to the bone.

Moe's sister was a professional hairdresser. She took one look at me, took me into the bathroom, and proceeded to shampoo my hair. With my hair set in curlers, I was put under a commercial hairdryer. Norman was whisked upstairs. At 5:30, neighbours appeared, stripped the kitchen table, and brought in casseroles and other assorted bowls of food. Others set the extended table with tablecloths, dishes, cutlery, wine, and flowers. Moe's sister and mother dressed me in a royal blue suit, my white blouse, and a veiled hat that Moe's mother had bought in Paris. Four men set up the *chupah* (wedding canopy). The wedding began.

For a moment, I didn't recognize Norman as he descended the stairs. I had never seen him in a suit or a hat before. *Who is this man?* I began to panic. *What am I doing!* I was operating on automatic pilot. As I was eating and drinking among total strangers, it felt hard to believe that I had just been married. Nevertheless, it was a beautiful gesture by a community of strangers who wholeheartedly and generously performed the Jewish *mitzvah* (good deed) of making a wedding for a poor young couple.

We lived for a short time in Toronto, and once again I postponed my university studies. Norman could not find work, so we moved to Montreal, where he hoped to have better luck. Norman found a tedious minimum-wage job in a machine shop. He longed to return to Israel.

"Working merely for money just doesn't do it for me. I need to be a part of something more meaningful. Maybe we need to go back to Israel. What do you think, Gloria?"

"I don't know, Norm. You've hardly given North American life a chance. Let's sleep on it."

Norman was an autodidact. When he was 12, his school in Birmingham, England, was bombed, which put an end to his formal education. He was a voracious reader with a phenomenal memory. While I was a linear, logical thinker, Norman was a lateral, intuitive, creative thinker. His thinking both fascinated and frustrated me. Nevertheless, I loved his strong independent moral core and admired his sense of autonomy. He danced to his own tune.

While we were living in Montreal, Norman took the college entrance exams and was granted admission to the University of Iowa. We put down a deposit for student-couples' housing. Our lives were becoming more goal oriented and future directed. We both began to hope.

Life was a mixture of both contentment and dissatisfaction as we became more acquainted with each other's American and British culture. We spent several Saturday afternoons on the campus of McGill University watching West Indians play cricket. Norman liked a pint of beer and introduced me to lamb with mint sauce, steak-and-kidney pie, and Cockney rhyming slang. We both loved the British films produced by J. Arthur Rank. Politics and Israel were constant topics of discussion. We argued vehemently about the best avenues to political change. Was Gandhi's civil disobedience more effective and moral than violent revolution? We bantered back and forth about my academic jargon and his colourful straightforward speech. Norman could make me laugh with his dry ironic sense of humour. Growing together was challenging but highly satisfying.

In August, 1952, Norman received a notice to attend a hearing at the American consulate in Montreal, where he was informed that he was not eligible to enter the United States. No reasons were given and no appeal was possible. The door to our future had just been slammed shut; our dreams were shattered. During the McCarthy period, it was a time of red-baiting and blacklisting. It was a critical turning point in our lives.

"Norm, what should we do?"

"I'm not sure. My friend, Noel, lives in Vancouver now. He was in the tanks with me in Israel. He is working as a CBC radio announcer. He always talked about Vancouver as 'God's country.' Perhaps we should go out there. I'll tell you what. Let's toss a coin. Heads, we go west to Vancouver. Tails, we go east to Israel."

Heads won, and that is how major life decisions are sometimes made — by the toss of a coin.

We took the train across Canada and arrived in Vancouver on a beautiful fall day. The colourful North Shore Mountains and waterways framed the city. This spacious city with its many expansive tree-lined streets felt open and welcoming. For $32 per month, we found a furnished one-room bed-sitter with a small kitchenette on the top floor of a house on Tenth Ave. and Spruce St. We both earned $20 per hour modelling nude at the

Vancouver School of Art, when we could get the work. We were resourceful and resilient.

Encouraged by his success at having passed the American college entrance exams, Norman decided to study for his British Columbia junior and senior matriculation, completing the two-year program in one year. Although he passed five of the eight subjects, because some were at a lower level and others at a higher level, he achieved neither a junior nor a senior matriculation. Disheartened and disappointed, he abandoned his pursuit of an academic path.

Instead, Norman joined an exciting writers' group, which became an important outlet for his creativity. Some of the writers included Robert and Marge Harlow, Bill McConnell, and Ben Maartman, all of whom became well-known names on the BC literary scene.

Money was very tight. Eventually Norman got a job at CBC, striking television sets. Soon after, he began working on the waterfront as a longshoreman. Work was very sporadic and after a year and a half, our average monthly income was a mere $75. We struggled to survive financially. I continued my course work at the University of Iowa by correspondence. By working part-time as a waitress and art model, I managed to keep us afloat.

Norman could not seem to find a direction. Civilian life in Canada confounded him. In England, he would have gone to the labour exchange and found work. In Canada, this occurred mainly through a network of connections. His first response was to shut down emotionally. Confused and frustrated, I struggled with this initial reaction. We were both unhappy, unable to communicate, and too paralyzed to act.

Our very first home was a shack in the tiny hamlet of Dollarton on the North Shore, between Vancouver and Deep Cove. Norman paid $250 for it in the spring of 1954. It stood on pilings below the theoretical high tide mark, the maximum height that it might possibly rise. Waterways were under the jurisdiction of the federal government. We did not own any of the land. We were literally squatters!

The shack consisted of three rooms: a bedroom, kitchen, and another undesignated room. It had a large wraparound veranda that offered a magnificent view of Burrard Inlet, but no running water, electricity, toilet or bathing facilities, and no refrigeration. We owned a portable radio, a double bed, a table, four chairs, and a wood stove for cooking and heating, but no dry wood!

That summer was cold and rainy, and the roof leaked. I put pots in various places on the floor to catch the drips from the ceiling. I was pregnant with my first child, constantly nauseated, and lost 15 pounds in the first three months of my pregnancy. To escape the hideous reality of my circumstances, I once stayed in bed for an entire week, huddled underneath an eiderdown quilt, which my grandmother had given me when I first left home, reading *War and Peace*. Norman attracted interesting and unusual acquaintances and our cottage was always open to stimulating and exciting people: longshoremen, writers, travelers, and students.

Four shacks over lived Malcolm Lowry, the world-famous author of *Under the Volcano*, and his wife, Margery. An alcoholic remittance man, Malcolm received regular monthly cheques from his wealthy family to stay out of England. Malcolm and I spent many an afternoon talking about his childhood and the rejection by his parents, as well as my dilemma of my unwanted pregnancy and dire poverty. He understood and was attuned to human suffering like no other person I have ever met. Norman and I made Malcolm's forty-third birthday party in our shack in June. It was an uproarious alcoholic affair. Malcolm and Margery left for England shortly thereafter.

Life hit a new low point for me. Our lives had become so precarious, I wasn't sure I would keep the baby or give it up for adoption. In September, Norman and I rented a tiny but charming house two miles down the highway in Cove Cliff. It was a three-room summer cottage with a real kitchen, electricity and a full-flush bathroom. We were finally living like ordinary people.

On January 23, 1955, I gave birth to David Ron, seven pounds, eight ounces. I was overwhelmed with love for him and bursting with joyful euphoria. I realized how precious was this gift I had just been given. Norman and I discovered a common love object and began to centre our lives around our baby. Unfortunately, our landlady did not want to rent to a family with children and gave us notice to move.

I was determined to acquire a permanent shelter for our baby, and was convinced that we needed to own something. We began to explore the possibilities of ownership in Deep Cove. By selling my piano in New Jersey for $250 dollars to my friend, Rhea, and the shack in Dollarton to Ben Maartman for $250, we managed to scrabble together a down payment of $500 for a small summer cottage in Deep Cove, with a mortgage of $2,500. Our monthly mortgage payments were $45.

The 750-square-foot house stood on a 50 by 120 foot lot. Its foundations were merely posts on concrete footings, with no basement. The house had two bedrooms, a living room, a tiny bathroom (with a toilet, sink and a shower stall with a rotting floor), a kitchen with a converted-to-oil Aga stove and a built-in red-upholstered dining nook, and a large enclosed porch with wraparound windows. It was light, cheerful, and welcoming. We loved it. As new homeowners, we felt like millionaires.

Through a friend, Norman eventually found steady employment as a youth worker in the Vancouver Juvenile Detention Home. A quick learner, he absorbed the required skills almost immediately. He had excellent innate interpersonal abilities plus deep empathy and an intuitive sense of psychological boundaries. He thrived on the challenge.

When David was six months old, I became pregnant again. Tamar Leah was born on April 14, 1956. She was the very opposite of David — a contented baby. Tamar had a serene and placid temperament and loved to sleep. The sheer pleasure of nursing her for six months created a very special bond. To top it off, she was a gorgeous blue-eyed blond, with a peaches-and-cream complexion. Her looks made me wonder where she came from.

Norman and I renewed our commitment to each other and to our future as a family. We worked together to build our nest, constantly renovating, improving, turning the cottage into a more substantial house. We had two beautiful lively children whom we both adored. Our social circle was diverse and interesting. Norman enjoyed his work and found it stimulating. We were both grateful for a regular steady income. I finally felt safe, loved, and contented.

Then one day, Norman, not wanting to get too complacent, said, "Gloria, what about going back to Israel?"

Startled, I replied, "Really? You want to go back to Israel?"

"I feel good about what we have here. Now, I know I can make it in Canada. But I have this itch. It's for a tiny country, called Israel, with a big dream. I need to at least give it a real go."

"Me, too. I didn't want to say much. I thought it would unsettle you. But I, too, dream about Israel. I have such a deep love for that country. Norm, yes! Let's do it.

I'm so excited." His words had awakened a deep unconscious yearning inside of me and I gave him a gigantic hug.

We spent the summer packing, purchasing necessities to take with us, organizing the trip, and planning our future with the help of the Jewish Agency, known as the *Sochnut* in Israel. We leased our house to a reliable young couple and in mid-September 1957, Norman, David, Tamar and I sailed from New York to Haifa on the S.S. Tsion.

CHAPTER 3

Arrival

Breathes there a man, with soul so dead,
Who never to himself hath said,
This is my own, my native land!
Whose heart hath ne'er within him burn'd.
As home his footsteps he hath turn'd
From wandering on a foreign strand!
— Sir Walter Scott, "Breathes There a Man"

We arrived in Israel during the third week of September, on a late afternoon. Shimon brought the settlement's truck to meet us at the Haifa dock. After going through customs and immigration, we boarded the truck with our mountain of possessions and headed for Kfar Daniel, a *meshek shitufi* (modified kibbutz), in central Israel. We preferred settling in the central part of Israel, and had refused to go to a more isolated settlement in the Negev, in the deep south of Israel.

A petite, slender young mother with short wavy dark-brown hair and large hazel eyes alight with anticipation, I looked out excitedly at the countryside. After so many years of yearning, I was once again in the land of my dreams, and the dreams of my beloved grandmother and father. This time, I was coming here to stay, to fulfill my dream.

At 16, I had joined Habonim, a Labour-Zionist youth organization, in Brooklyn. I had read about the early pioneers and their inspiring leadership. I knew its history and much of its literature. Since my father had given an Orthodox Jewish education only to my brothers, I hadn't begun learning Hebrew until my first year at university when, linguistically gifted, I poured myself into learning the language. As I looked out the window of the truck, it was hard for me to believe that I was once again in this sacred land.

Norman looked straight ahead. He told me he was thinking about the adjustment that lay ahead of us. He was a committed secularist. His father was his hero and had been an active card-carrying member of the Communist Party in Britain. However, as an adventurer and a former soldier, Norman had volunteered to fight in the Israeli War of Independence. It was still a time of high idealism and excitement and Norman felt committed to building a just and compassionate society. This, indeed, was a land he could believe in.

Our two children sat quietly between us. David, with brown hair and brown eyes, was a sturdy rambunctious nearly three-year-old. Blond, blue-eyed and fair, Tamar, at nearly two years of age, was a quiet, more self-contained child. They were probably wondering where they were going and what they were going to do there.

To ease the absorption into a new land, most newcomers were placed on settlements with others who spoke the same language. Kfar Daniel was considered an *"anglo-saxim"* settlement, because most of the residents came from English-speaking countries, the majority from South Africa, England, Canada, and the United States, and a few from India and Malaysia. Many spoke Hebrew with a heavy Cockney accent, which was quite hilarious.

David and Tamar were getting restless and cranky in the truck. I managed to distract them with cookies and juice. As we arrived at the settlement, known simply as the *meshek*, Shimon drove the truck along the lower row of houses and stopped at a small square house, faced in large gold-coloured Jerusalem stone. We descended from the truck, stopped, and gazed at this dwelling for a moment. Approaching, we took a deep breath, and then opened the door to our new home, to our life's new adventure.

We entered immediately into the dining-kitchen area, with its basic table and four chairs. On the table was a large handwritten sign in Hebrew and in English saying "Bruchim Habayim — Welcome." The kitchen had a sink and a counter with curtained shelves below. The shelves were stocked with a *ptilia* (paraffin cooker), a few pots and pans, a *seer peleh* (wonder pot), a basic set of four dishes and glasses, and a few potatoes, carrots, and onions. To the side was an icebox stuffed with oranges, milk, bread, tomatoes, cucumbers, olives, eggs, soft white cheese and several soured milk products, like yoghurt and sour cream. Two loaves of rye bread stood on the counter.

"Mama, pee, pee," said David. I looked around and found a small shower room and a toilet room but neither was operational. Shimon explained that they weren't yet connected to the sewage system and directed me to the nearest outhouse. Opposite the utilities rooms was the children's bedroom with two single beds and two small chests of drawers.

Several members of the *meshek* greeted us warmly and assisted in the unloading of our possessions. An attractive medium-built -woman with wavy blond hair and a fair complexion walked over from the next house with a cake, and introduced herself in a very clipped British accent. "Hello, I'm Dorothy Black, your neighbour. That's Basil, my husband, carrying one of your boxes. Welcome to Kfar Daniel. You must be very tired. Why don't you bring your little ones over to my place, have a cup of tea, and let the men handle the rest of the unloading."

Norman turned around and said, "That's a good idea. It's okay, Gloria. Take the kids and go. I know you need it. We'll manage just fine here. Thanks, Dorothy."

Holding my two children by the hand, I reluctantly followed Dorothy to a house identical to ours. In the living room, a four-year-old boy sat on the floor playing with wooden building blocks. David immediately rushed over to join him.

"Hi, I'm David. Can I have some blocks? I can build a tower."

"Okay. But only the yellow ones. I need all the others. I'm Ephraim."

Soon the two boys were busily chatting away like old friends. Tamar climbed on my lap and clung tightly to me. Dorothy put a steaming pot of tea, milk, sugar and cookies on the table and sat down. "Where are you from in Canada? What do you do? Tell me something about yourself." We chatted for about twenty-five minutes. I was pleased to have made a friend. Finally, Dorothy said, "You might want to bring your kids to the pre-school tomorrow morning. What do you think?"

"I don't know. This has all been so strange for them."

"Yes, but look at your son now. He immediately gravitated to play with another child. He seems like such a delightfully outgoing child."

"But Tamar is still a baby. She is not like that."

"Well, keep her home for another day or two. We usually take the children to the *gan* (pre-school) just before 8:30. Phillip, that is Ephraim in Hebrew, will show David the way home at noon. I'll knock on your door and we can go up there together. Tomorrow is Wednesday, the day we get our chickens for the week. After we drop off David and Phillip, we can continue to the *tsarchania* and pick out our chickens."

"*Tsarchania?* What's that?"

"Our general store. You'll get a budget that will be paid to you in coupons, *t'lushim*, and then you can buy whatever you need from the store. I'll show you tomorrow."

Basil entered the house and said, "All your stuff's now unloaded. I'm not trying to rush you or anything. But you might want to return to your house to feed your kids and put them to bed."

"Thank you so much, both of you. Yes, it's time I took these kids home." I got up, carried Tamar, gathered David and walked back to our new house. All our possessions were indeed inside the house but there were boxes everywhere and chaos reigned. Norman, I, and even the children worked feverishly for another hour until a semblance of order emerged.

Our even-tempered Tamar whined and fussed. I quickly made an Israeli supper of yoghurt and soft white cheese, a diced salad of tomato, cucumber, green pepper seasoned with garlic, salt and pepper, olive oil and lemon juice, accompanied by delicious rye bread. They each had a piece of Dorothy's cake with a glass of milk and ate with gusto. Equilibrium was restored. Norman and I washed the children at the kitchen sink and put them to bed. Norman read them *Make Way for Ducklings*, their favorite book, and they fell fast asleep.

Norman and I resumed unpacking linens, clothing, pots and pans, dishes, books, and a radio. I made a fresh pot of tea and we listened to the BBC Radio news. We talked about the day and how it had unfolded, and discussed plans for the next day and our feelings for Israel.

"We made it!" I exclaimed exultantly. "You know, when I was 16, I dreamed about living in a country where the policemen were Jewish, not Irish, where I would go to school and not be 'the other' and have to recite the 'Lord's Prayer' every morning. And here I am! I'm *so* happy."

"C'mon, *Chabeebati*, (my beloved), let's go to bed. You look absolutely exhausted."

We climbed into bed, cuddling together, weary and happy. So ended our first night back in Israel.

When I opened one eye and looked at the clock, it was 5:50 a.m. and the room was flooded with light from a cloudless azure sky. Norman knew the drill. He rose, washed quickly, pulled on his shorts, t-shirt, hat and sandals and was out the door to join the other men descending to the fields. I rolled over to get another hour of sleep.

David and Tamar awakened at 7:00 a.m. and began exploring their new home. They soon discovered two small lizards clinging to the screen on their window, which they promptly dubbed Berl and Shmerl. They investigated the toilet room and couldn't understand why the flush handle did not produce water. Or why the taps were also dry in the shower room. Bored, they shook me awake and said they were hungry. I gave them both hugs and rose to welcome the day. We all washed at the kitchen sink and dressed. I made a typical Israeli breakfast, which closely resembled the previous night's supper. The children ate all their food with relish.

At 8:15, Dorothy appeared at the door with Ephraim. "Are you ready to go to the *gan*?"

"We're ready." I said.

Ephraim quickly left his mother to walk beside David. As we approached the pre-school, I noticed a playground with swings, slides, seesaw, and a big sandbox, several shovels, pails, boxes of various sizes, and littered with lots of exploratory junk. Several shade trees stood around the perimeter. Off to the side of the playground was a long low rectangular building of golden Jerusalem stone, with a bright red door and red window trims.

At the pre-school, Dorothy introduced us to Esther, the slim, attractive *ganenet* (teacher). "Esther, this is Gloria, Galila, from Canada; a new immigrant, an *olah chadasha*, and her children, David and Tamar."

"*Naim m'od. Brucha haba'ah.* It's a pleasure to meet you. Welcome. Your children will be in good hands."

"David, say *shalom* to Esther," I prompted. "She will be your new teacher."

"*Shalom.* Can I go now and play with Ephraim?"

"You can after I introduce you to the class," said Esther. "*Yeledim, hinei yeled chadash sh'yikanes l'kita. Tagid, shalom, oo'varuch habah.* (Children, here is a new child who will join the class. Tell him 'welcome.')"

The class responded, *"Shalom oo'varuch habah,"* and David and Ephraim raced over to the others at the jungle gym.

Tamar held on tightly to my hand while she observed the scene before her. Esther quickly sensed Tamar's cautiousness and called over a quiet, sweet two-year-old girl. "Nomi, would you like to show Tamar all the things you make in the sandbox?" Esther asked her in English. Nomi offered Tamar her hand. As the two little girls slowly drifted over to the sandbox, Tamar kept looking over her shoulder to see if I was still there.

"Thank you, Esther. I think they'll be okay now."

"Don't worry. If they should really need you, I will arrange to get them back to you."

I turned to watch Tamar, who had quickly become engrossed in making mud pies with Nomi, her new friend. I quickly walked away with Dorothy. As we walked ahead, Dorothy pointed out a low squat building. "That's the *tsarchania.* Sonia runs it. She has no children, so she has to work five hours a day for the *meshek.* This particular work suits her. She's married to Richard, a former Queen's Guardsman, and he never lets you forget it. You know, the ones with the red jackets and tall beaver hats who stand in front of Buckingham Palace. Did you make a list of what you need?"

"Yes, I did. But I don't know how much I can spend because we don't have our budget yet."

"Basil is the treasurer so he can come over tonight and inform both of you. You don't want to buy too much because we have to carry our three chickens."

In the store, Sonia greeted us in very precise, proper English with a tinge of a foreign accent. "Welcome to Kfar Daniel. You're from Canada? How charming. I'm here to help you. You'll pick up your bread in the evening when you go to the *Bet Ha-Am* (general meeting hall) at the top of the hill for your work assignment. What would you like here?"

"'We can't carry too much, Sonia," said Dorothy. "We have to get our chickens. Put us down for three each. Galila, let's go outside and see what chickens we'll take."

I followed Dorothy to the side of the *tsarchania* to see a wall of birdcages, with live loud clucking chickens. Startled beyond my imagination, I could not say a word. Dorothy reached inside a cage, pressed her fingers against the underside of the bird and exclaimed, "Ooh, this one feels reasonably fat. Let's take this one." She grabbed the bird by the feet and pulled it out of the cage. I could hardly believe my eyes. "Here, hold her by her feet," Dorothy commanded, as she thrust the bird into my hand. "I'll find two more for you and we'll tie them all together."

Twenty minutes later, we walked down the familiar path, homeward bound, carrying three live chickens each! The birds were constantly trying to reach upward and nip my hand. I had always been both idealistic and pragmatic, but this was different. *What the hell am I doing here? These goddam birds scare the hell out of me.*

When we arrived home, Dorothy showed me how to tie the end of the rope around a tree to let the birds right themselves with limited ambulation. "When Norman comes home for lunch, he can kill them. You should pluck all three of them while they are still warm so the feathers don't get stuck."

Traumatized, I entered my new house, sat down, and just breathed. *Am I going to be able to do this? What was I thinking!* Gradually, I began to calm down and see the humour in the situation. "So, you wanted to be a *chalutza* (a pioneer)," I said to myself aloud, "so kill the goddam chickens and pluck them!"

I got up and began setting the table for the mid-day meal. David and Tamar burst into the house. "There's chickens in our yard," David exclaimed excitedly. "Can we play with them?"

"No, David, they are for eating. *Abba* will come home for dinner soon and he will kill them and then I will pluck off all the feathers and cook them for our dinners. We have to be grateful for these chickens that will give us our food for this week."

David paused and said scornfully, "That's okay. I didn't think they would make such good pets anyway."

Tamar started to cry, "Why do we have to *kill* them? Won't it hurt them? I don't like it when I hurt or something hurts. I'm scared."

33

I cuddled Tamar on my lap. "Tamar, we try to kill them in a way that causes the least hurt. We need them. They give us food. *Abba* will kill them outside. You can stay inside with me and we'll do something special while he does it."

"I'm not afraid," David said, proudly pushing out his chest. "I'll stay out there with *Abba*. I'll help him."

When Norman arrived, I handed him a sharp knife and turned away. Within minutes, three beheaded birds were prancing around our front lawn until they dropped. I shuddered and could hardly look out the window. Finally, the ordeal was over. Ironically, after a few months, this weekly event became completely normal. Every Wednesday, as soon as David spotted Norman coming home for dinner, he would rush out to hand his father the knife for the slaughter.

Our family ate dinner, our main meal, at mid-day. Then we all lay down on our beds for a siesta. It was the hottest time of the day. Israel has many climate zones. Kfar Daniel lay east of the southern tip of the coastal plain and its dry heat was hotter and lasted longer than in other central parts of the country. The hot summers and falls were especially trying.

After siesta, Norman went down to the fields once again to move heavy irrigation pipes. I put the chickens in boiling water to make the removal of the feathers easier and began plucking.

At four o'clock, Norman returned and we all headed to the *Miklachat,* the common shower room. Norman took David to the men's side and I took Tamar to the women's section. While showering with other women, all sense of modesty or shame dissolved in the awareness of the many different sizes and shapes of the human body. Instead, it became a time of gossip, camaraderie and light-heartedness.

Upon our return home, we were invited to four o'clock tea at Yishai and Mahrie's house, just above Dorothy's. Their children, Layah and David, 6 and 4, were considerably older than Tamar and David but they played together with ease. Mahrie and Yishai were a warm-hearted, welcoming couple. They came from working-class parents in Manchester and had thick Midland accents. Hebrew was a difficult language for both of them. Mahrie was a very kind outgoing young woman who greatly missed her orderly English way of life. She often spoke of missing her home, meeting girlfriends in tea rooms, and eating fried kippers for breakfast.

We soon learned that one of Yishai's jobs was to drive the tractor with a large attached wagon once a week around Kfar Daniel and empty all the garbage stations on the settlement into the wagon. The garbage was later buried in a specially designed pit. Consequently, he was able to surmise from the garbage who had recently received a food parcel from South Africa, who was still menstruating, who had a gift from America. Privacy and confidentiality were a rarity on Kfar Daniel. It was like a small village. There was no such thing as anonymity.

Yishai was a great gossip, with few boundaries as to what was appropriate. Laced with a rollicking sense of humour, his tales were generally benign and therefore tolerated. Afternoon tea at Mahrie and Yishai's was always light-hearted and filled with laughter.

After a light supper, David and Norman walked up to the *Bet Ha-Am*. David felt very important being there with his *Abba*. As a newcomer, Norman did not have a permanent work assignment. He was considered a *p'cock*, a cork, since he floated from job to job. The aspiration of every member was to have a permanent placement. Although Norman had been a mechanic and worked on tractors, he had to bide his time. He collected the bread for the next day and slowly walked hand in hand with David down the hill to our home.

When the children were finally in bed, Norman and I had a moment to relax. We had brought a compact motel-size combination fridge and stove from Canada. It was the latest model but it was not yet hooked up. I pointed to the paraffin camp cooker. "I can't keep cooking on something as primitive as a *p'tilia*. We need to get our Canadian gas cook stove hooked up and in place."

"You're right," Norman agreed. "I'll ask the men who to phone, and I'll go up to the office before I come home for dinner tomorrow. I'll make the arrangements. Don't worry. Before you know it, you'll be cooking on a proper stove. I promise."

"At least the fridge part is plugged in and I don't have to use the icebox. I put all the chickens in the fridge."

We listened to the regular ten o'clock BBC news. Then Norman said, "C'mon *Chabeebi*, you must be wiped out. I know I am. We've completed our first full day at Kfar Daniel. Time to go to sleep.

CHAPTER 4

Adapting

Believing means liberating the indestructible element in oneself,
or, more accurately, liberating oneself, or, more accurately,
being indestructible, or, more accurately, being.
—— Franz Kafka, *The Blue Octavo Notebooks* (1954)

The next day, shortly after noon, Norman returned, a grim look on his face. "Luv, the gas company won't provide us with gas unless we buy *their* stove, which amounts to a thousand lira."

"That's outrageous. Isn't there another company we can get gas from?"

"Nope. This is Israel and they have a monopoly."

"What can we do? This is awful."

"I know. I'm so sorry."

"What did the others do?"

"Many knew ahead of time and planned for it. The cost was less 10 years ago when they were setting up."

My pragmatism and bravado came to the fore. "No! I won't give those bastards the satisfaction of fleecing us. And, I don't think we should start our lives here in debt. I'll manage." I said fiercely.

"Are you sure? I've asked a lot of you and I want you to be happy."

"I am happy. I have you and the kids and a country I love. It will be okay. Let's eat and then we can sleep on it."

So, I learned to cook and make delicious meals on a *p'tilia* and a primus, a paraffin burner that I had to pump. The primus gave a more intense heat. Since they were small camp stoves, they were safest on the floor, so I squatted to cook my meals. I also became adept at using the *seer peleh,* truly a wonder pot, in which I would bake a cake, roast potatoes or make a host of other goodies.

By late afternoon, I had let go of my anger and resentment. Perhaps we should have checked in advance with the *Sochnut* about a stove. As I began to reconcile to the situation, I felt better. This was my life and I could do it.

That evening, after the children were in bed, I sat outside on the lawn and looked up at the dark velvety sky. The huge stars seemed to hang so very low. I felt I could almost reach up and touch them. Silence and peace permeated the air. I began to sing "Veyulai" (Perhaps), which captured the longing of the poetess, Rachel.

> And perhaps, it was never so
> And perhaps, I never woke up and at the break
> of dawn
> To labour by the sweat of my brow
> And perhaps, on top of the wagon laden with
> sheaves
> It made my voice ring with song

Nor bathed myself clean in the calm blue water
of my Kinneret
Oh my Kinneret, Oh my Kinneret
Were you there, or did I merely dream it?

I sang of my values so beautifully expressed by the poet Saul Tshernachovsky's "Sachki, Sachki" (Laugh, Laugh at My Dreams).

Laugh, laugh at all my dreams
What I dream shall yet come true
Laugh at my belief in man
As I still believe in you.

The songs kept pouring out of me. I loved the language. I loved the earthiness of the life. I loved the dream I was living.

Yes, life was strange and at times difficult, but I felt deeply rooted to this land, to its history, to its heroes. I felt at home. I thought of my grandmother who had kept a vial of soil from Israel in one of her drawers, to ensure she would be buried with soil from the Holy Land.

Gradually, life fell into a pattern. Norman left at six o'clock and went down to the fields. The children awoke, washed and dressed at seven o'clock. Norman joined us and we all sat down for a hearty Israeli breakfast at 7:45. After breakfast, Norman returned to the fields. Finally, I was ready to take David and Tamar to the *gan,* and then I went to my work.

The hours of work assigned to the women were based on the number and ages of their children. Unlike childless Sonya, who worked five hours for the *meshek,* I, with two children aged two and three, owed the *meshek* only two hours of work per day. The rest of my time was attributed to my need to care for my children and manage my household.

My two hours consisted of cleaning five of the *meshek*'s 10 outhouses, which took about 25 minutes per outhouse. It was considered the lowest status job one could have. Most people grumbled when assigned this job. Being a newcomer, it was logical that I was assigned to do this work, which I accepted with equanimity.

Imagine my surprise when I discovered that "The Fair Rotation of Outhouse Cleaning" was the main topic on the agenda of the next general meeting. General meetings were held every Saturday evening. Norman and I decided to attend. Dorothy offered to keep her ears open and periodically look in on David and Tamar. When we arrived at the *Bet Ha-am*, there were two couples and six other individuals, which barely constituted a quorum. The total number of people eligible to vote was 57.

The meeting was called to order by Yossi Schlein, *Mazkir Ha-Hanhala,* Secretary of the Executive. Yossi was slight, of medium height, with sandy hair and blue eyes. He had a rather acerbic tongue and spoke with a distinct South African accent. He was one of the founding members of Kfar Daniel and had been its head since inception. I later learned that people often referred to him derisively as "Mr. Bet Chever." Bet Chever was the *meshek*'s official Hebrew name. The original Arab village was called Kafr Daniel, and the members tended to refer to the *meshek* by its original Arabic name.

After expeditiously dealing with a few housekeeping items, we came to the main issue on the agenda, the fair rotation of the outhouses. Aharon, known on the *meshek* to be a die-hard ideologue, stood up to speak. "I move that the work of cleaning the outhouses be rotated equally among *all* the *chaverim* (members) on the *meshek*. That is my motion. Now I wish to speak to my motion." He paused. "Let us not denigrate the work of cleaning the outhouses. We have to realize that there is dignity in *all* labour. Everyone on Kfar Daniel should have to take a turn in the cleaning. Do we really think that all those people who work upstairs in the offices should never dirty their hands?" Informally, people who worked in the offices and on the hill were often referred to as *tarbutnikim* (culturists), whereas those who worked down in the fields were referred to as *chamorim* (donkeys). Aharon continued. "The well-known Second Aliyah philosopher and leader, Alef Dal-ed Gordon, once said, 'The Land of Israel is acquired through labour, not through fire and not through blood.'"

Thus began the high-flown rhetoric of the debate. Several people got up to speak about the impracticality of the situation. Aharon once again orated loudly, quoting Gordon. "We must create a new people, a humane people, whose attitude toward other peoples is informed with the sense of human brotherhood and

42

whose attitude toward nature and all within it is inspired by noble urges of life-loving creativity."

People raised their voices. They pontificated, debated, argued and shouted. Heated discussions followed. Yossi tried in vain to keep order. Much principled, lofty rhetoric was expressed. The meeting lasted an hour and a half. The motion was defeated. Norman and I left the meeting shaking our heads. Paraphrasing Hannah Arendt's *The Banality of Evil*, I quipped, "The banality of the democratic process is overwhelming." We did not go to many meetings after that.

Ironically, I discovered that cleaning the outhouses was one of the easiest and most satisfying of jobs. It was mindless work. I was my own boss, I had full autonomy, starting when it was convenient for me, and often finishing in just an hour and a half, even when doing the job thoroughly and conscientiously. *Who cares about its status!* I told myself.

As newcomers to the settlement, we received a flurry of invitations to four o'clock teas. Families with young children tended not to go out in the evening. Since the days started early and were long, people tended to socialize around tea-time, after showering at the *Miklachat.*

Shula and Tsvi completed our inner social circle in our area. The couple lived on the other side of Dorothy and directly below Mahrie and Yishai. Shula was a quiet, soft-spoken slip of a woman, the daughter of an

43

Orthodox rabbi in London. As a committed secularist, she had broken away from all organized religion. Shula was an avid reader and had an incisive mind. Tsvi was a highly educated, dedicated Zionist who had studied agriculture. He had a profound love of the land and was committed to the development of the orchards of plums and apricots. He also had a very wry sense of humour. They had three sons, Daniel, Yoram and Ilan. Yoram was closest to David's age and became one of his closest buddies.

This couple was truly the backbone of Kfar Daniel. Grounded in practical agricultural knowledge, Jewish history and tradition, and completely non-judgmental, they were highly respected. They offered sage advice and were natural leaders. They read and spoke Hebrew fluently, reading both the daily *Ha-aretz* and *HaDavar*, the Labour Party newspaper. Political debate was always informative and lively in their house. We soon became fast friends.

The latest news talk revolved around the Israelis who foolishly wandered, got lost on the Jordanian side and were imprisoned. Markers rarely delineated the borders. Several individuals got lost in the desert. Each incident became a *cause célèbre*, causing much tension and anxiety. Fortunately, most incidents resulted in a release by the Jordanian authorities.

David and Tamar were adapting quickly. They eagerly rushed to the *gan* every morning. They loved Esther, the *ganenet*. It took only a matter of weeks before they were speaking to everyone in Hebrew. I decided to speak to the children in Hebrew, while Norman spoke to them in English. They answered both of us in Hebrew. However, when a new child entered the *gan,* they were able to translate the Hebrew around them to English for the newcomer. They moved easily between both languages without hesitation. David seemed to need and have many friends. Tamar was content with one "best friend," Yael's daughter, Nomi. They played side by side, occasionally talking to each other.

I observed and marveled at how their self-confidence grew in the loving security of the *meshek.* They understood they had to walk only on the established paths because there could be snakes under rocks. Aside from that warning, they were free to roam anywhere among the houses. If David did not arrive home for the mid-day meal, I knew that he must have stopped at a friend's house and that he was totally safe and cared for. They were at home everywhere. All *meshek* children were truly cherished. That was the profound joy that a sense of community provided.

Early one Monday morning in October, Norman received notice to report by the end of the week to the mobilization station in Tel Aviv for his *miluim* (annual month-long reserve duty). We were shocked.

When we arrived in Israel at the Haifa port a few weeks earlier, the authorities had asked Norman if he had ever served in the Israeli army and he had replied in the affirmative. He had been a volunteer in the Israeli

Defense Forces from 1948 to 1949 and again in 1950. They immediately pulled out a huge book, opened it to the L's and found his name. They read, "Levi, Norman sergeant, 1950." Turning to Norman, they asked him in Hebrew, "Levi Norman 1950, where have you been all these years?" To which Norman replied, "Abroad." Having left the country without authorization, Norman had been demoted to trooper. Now, in 1957, he was returning as a trooper to do his duty.

Norman lightly packed his rucksack and slung it over his shoulder. David, Tamar and I walked up the hill with him to the *Bet Ha-am*, where the truck was waiting to take him into Tel Aviv. We kissed, hugged and said goodbye. The truck began to move and Tamar started to cry as we began to slowly walk down to our house. We didn't hear from Norman for six days before we finally received a letter. He wrote:

> We are somewhere deep in the desert preparing for maneuvers with tanks. It is amazing to see men from so many different parts of the country assemble and in such a short time turn into efficient working squadrons.
>
> David and Tamar, I miss you both very much and count the days when I will see you. I will get one Shabbat, the Shabbat following the next one, in which I will probably be able to get home on a Friday evening. Chabeebi, I'm counting the days.
>
> All my love,
> *Abba*, Norman

We waited and counted the days. Life felt surreal without their *Abba*. Finally, the awaited Friday arrived. We cleaned the house until it sparkled. I cooked a special Shabbat dinner. Norman came striding down the path, rucksack slung over his shoulder, his face darkened by the desert sun, 10 pounds thinner and looking very fit. David and Tamar clambered all over him, shouting, "*Abba, Abba.*" I looked at Norman with tears in my eyes and said, "We missed you." It was quite a celebration!

Shabbat morning! Peaceful ... restful ... beautiful, treasured time! Truly holy time. We awakened and breakfasted at a leisurely pace. We ate lots of green olives, soft white cheese, and the usual diced tomatoes, cucumbers and green peppers, followed by milk and delicious coffee cake. We went for a stroll through the neighbouring Herzl Forest, which wasn't a forest at all. It was actually several large groves of cypress and eucalyptus trees. In this brown arid land, green was a cherished colour. It warmed our hearts and fed our souls, and our dreams of what could be — what should be — a green fertile land.

Suddenly, we saw a porcupine with its quills extended. Norman shouted, "Don't go near, David. It can hurt you. Come here, now!" He and David stood quietly, then walked slowly around the creature and continued on. Norman explained to David and Tamar how the porcupine protected himself with his quills and how it was important not to frighten him. David wondered how it would feel to be hit with a quill. "Like being shot by an arrow," Norman replied. "Only this time there would be many arrows." "Ooh," said Tamar, "I wouldn't like that at all."

After lunch and siesta, I invited our neighbours over for tea. In honour of Norman's homecoming, I had successfully baked a second cake in my see*r peleh* and was eager to show off my newfound skill.

"My goodness, Norm," said Mahri, "you look 10 years younger."

"Credit it to the rigours of army service," said Norman.

"Last year, they had a general *giyoos* (mobilization) in the country, and half the country was called up," said Basil. "You never know when we might have to fight. Best to be prepared."

"I remember that very well," Dorothy chimed in. "The entire country was glued to their radios to find out if their number would be called. It was a terribly tense time." We all grew very quiet as we silently confronted the dangerous reality of our lives and what it all meant.

"Welcome to our life," said Yishai, his sarcasm obvious.

"I spent three years in the British army, but I've never known an army as well prepared as this one," said Norman. "Their organization is truly remarkable."

"I only hope we *never* have to use this knowledge and skill," I said fervently. The unspoken anxiety in the room was palpable. Then the talk turned to *meshek* gossip. Our friends left early and Norman prepared to

48

leave and go back to his army base. He packed his rucksack and gave each child a big hug and kisses. Norman turned to me and we kissed passionately. "Keep the home fires burning," he joked and walked out the door.

Being on my own was indeed a trial. David acted up more often. The evenings were lonely. Work was boring. I longed for the *miluim* to be over. Ten days after Norman's visit, Dorothy knocked on my door. "There's a call for you in the office. It's Norman. Hurry. I'll look after the kids."

Terrified, I dashed out the door and ran to the office. Panting heavily, I gasped, "Norm! Are you alright?"

"Hey, slow down there. Of course, I'm alright. I didn't mean to frighten you. I just wanted to give you a heads up. I'm being de-mobbed Sunday morning and should be back on the *meshek* by noon. I'll take buses and then a taxi from Lod."

"Oh, Norm, I can hardly wait. The kids miss you so much. Me, too. Are you sure you're alright?"

"'Course I'm alright. See you in four days. Take care, *Chabeebi.* I'll be home before you know it. Love you."

I slowly walked back to my house, hugging myself as I visualized Norman's return. I told the children that *Abba* would be home in four days. They jumped around, cheering and shouting with joy. As I put them to bed on Saturday night, I told them, "When you come home from *gan* tomorrow, *Abba* will be here." Contentment returned to the household once more.

49

Again, I baked a special cake. David and Tamar rushed home from pre-school. When Norman came striding down the hill, the children rushed out to climb all over him. It was another glorious homecoming.

Later that evening, Norman told me he had never experienced anything like that *miluim.* "Men came from every part of Israel. They did not know each other. Within five days of meeting, their units were high functioning and using live ammunition in all their maneuvers. Such super efficiency could never happen in the British Army. I'm glad I went but I'm sure glad to be back. I missed you. Hey, lighten up. It's okay. I'm not going anywhere."

"Of course not. Because I'm putting a ball and chain around you from now on." We laughed as we went to bed.

CHAPTER 5

Cooperative Farm Life

Where the mind is without fear and the head is held high
Where knowledge is free;
Where the walls have not been broken up into fragments by domestic walls;
Where words come out from the depths of truth;
Where tireless striving stretches its arms toward perfection:
Where the clear stream of reason has not lost its way into the dreary desert sand of dead habit;
Where the mind is led forward by thee into ever-widening thought and action.
— Rabindranath Tagore, "Where the Mind Is Without Fear"

Back again as a family unit, it was as though no interruption had occurred. The rainy season was beginning. Dorothy and I went to Hamashbir in Haifa to buy gumboots and rain gear for our children. It was the retail cooperative that provided consumer goods to *kibbutzim* and other cooperatives. Hamashbir was like a North American big-box store. When I checked out, I simply gave the cashier the name of Kfar Daniel and my member number and my purchases were credited to our account.

One Friday afternoon, the cloudless sky suddenly darkened. There was a loud clap of thunder and the heavens opened to a deluge driven by high winds. It poured sheets of water. The ground was completely drenched. An hour later, it was over — the first rain of the season! There was *botz* (mud), glorious *botz*, everywhere. The children happily marched in their gumboots through the mud.

For me, who was used to the gentle persistent drizzle of Vancouver, the dramatic rainfalls of Israel were astonishing. Every day, or every few days, we experienced dramatic cloudbursts that lasted an hour or two, followed by sunshine and a sparkling brightness. I could taste the delicious rainwater on my lips. Rain, water — the source of life in a hot dry climate. How appropriate that prayers for rain have a central place in Jewish prayer books. With the change in the weather, agricultural work diminished. I spent more time engaged with others.

Kfar Daniel had a great diversity of people. While living communally, people-watching was infinitely fascinating to me. Lives of others engrossed me. I instinctively liked people and enjoyed their company. Norman's and my delight in others was often reciprocated.

Yehudah and Rachel were Jews from India, who had settled in Kfar Daniel in 1950. They had two delightful teenage sons, Eytan and Michael, who were serious students in the high school in neighbouring Ben Shemen. Rachel worked upstairs in the office as secretary. Yehudah was the *raftan*, in charge of the dairy herd.

Yehudah was conscientious, hard working, and totally dedicated. Over the previous eight years, he had built up an outstanding herd of 40 cows. Big milk producers, they were known throughout the Galilee. He took great pride in the herd and in his achievement. However, when the *Sochnut* discovered that the entire country had an overproduction of dairy products, they decreed that those assets would be better reallocated to the expansion and development of egg production. Consequently, the *Sochnut* recommended that the *meshek* begin phasing out its herd.

Yehudah could barely comply. Dispirited, seeing his life's work being dismantled, he decided to leave the *meshek* and try his luck in Tel Aviv, where he had several close relatives. Coming from India and being dark-skinned, he had never felt totally integrated in the social life of the *meshek*. As an *anglo-saxim* settlement, subtle racism existed but was glossed over and unacknowledged.

Norman and I spent time with Yehudah and his family and witnessed the anxiety and fear that accompanied leaving this safe, comfortable, communal way of life. The family now had to worry about finding work and accommodation, the cost of living and schooling for their boys.

When a member leaves a kibbutz or a *meshek shitufi,* the other members see it as a massive rejection of their way of life. It is as if someone has attacked their religion. Suddenly, no one would speak to Yehudah or

Rachel, or even acknowledge them. They became *personae non gratae;* they were shunned and sent into exile. Yehudah and Rachel were devastated by this harsh treatment. They grew very silent and worked diligently as they prepared to leave. One day, one of their cousins arrived with a van, which they packed and filled. Only Norman and I came to see them off. We hugged and kissed, and exchanged addresses.

"It is so sad. I hate to see them go," I said to Norman as the van drove away. "Yehudah and Rachel are such good people and the *meshek* treated them shabbily. How could people be so nice and warm to Yehudah and Rachel and then turn on them the way they did?"

Norman put his arm around me and shook his head sadly. "That can be the cruelty of blind ideological belief." Those remarks puzzled me. I had spent so much of my young adult life reading ideological literature. Wasn't that where all my idealism had come from? Hadn't I been uplifted and inspired by noble great minds? Watching this so-called idealism play itself out gave me pause. At the same time, the joy of communal celebrations was beguiling.

Several weeks passed. Excitement filled the air. Paid workers had been busy at Kfar Daniel for a month. The rainy season was almost over. At long last, every household would have a functioning flush toilet and shower. No more outhouse cleaning! No more communal showers at the *Miklachat!* The day arrived when work on the last row of houses was finally completed. It was time to celebrate.

A committee decorated the *Bet Ha-Am*, the central meeting hall. The women baked, made salads, brought buns, fruit, and enticing appetizers. Children ran around laughing and shouting. We ate, drank, schmoozed, sang folk songs, and danced folk dances. Speeches were made. The atmosphere was filled with good will, a sense of achievement, pride, and fellowship. It was a grand celebration. Once again, Norman and I walked home feeling a deep sense of fulfillment and belonging. In such a short time, this place had truly become our home. We were Jews in a Jewish land.

As the weather began to change, I made plans to walk into Lod on my own, although I was still somewhat hesitant and fearful. Finally, I decided to take the two and a half mile-walk into Lod to purchase sandals and a blouse for myself, pipe tobacco for Norman, and a treat for the kids. This would be my first big solo adventure. Free for the afternoon, I strode through the Herzl forest, past the religious kibbutz, Gamzu, past the children's village of Ben Shemen, thoroughly enjoying myself. After another mile, I began to enter Lod.

The Biblical city of Lod had a tragic recent past. Jews were forced to leave during the Arab riots of 1921. In 1948, the Jews expelled all its Arab inhabitants — men, women children, the old and the very young. At the time, the Arabs were living peacefully and cooperatively with their Israeli neighbours. I was unaware that Ben Gurion had encouraged and urged expulsion wherever possible. Pictures of the cruel expulsion of thousands of Lod Arabs reminded me of timeless Jewish expulsions. It epitomized the ethical dilemma, and the price the Arabs had paid, in the establishment of a Jewish state. The town was resettled mainly by Jews who had been forced to flee from Arab countries.

Lod was an old, dusty neglected town of approximately 4,500. The west side of old Lod was developing a new modern quarter. Most of the inhabitants of old Lod lived in small, stone houses. Several small one-room synagogues were scattered along the side streets. In the long commercial main street that ran down the centre of town, I found the women's dress shop, selected a colourful floral blouse and began bargaining with the owner in Hebrew. Eventually we agreed upon a price and I left. I was elated. My Hebrew skills had advanced considerably and I was able to do the entire negotiation with ease in Hebrew. I quickly found the shoe store and purchased my sandals. Sweets and tobacco were easily found.

Most of the activity in the town occurred around the central bus station. There were many bus bays, where people were already lined up. Amidst the noise and bustle stood a small kiosk selling bus tickets. Three taxis were parked at a taxi stand. Lod was a link between Tel Aviv and Jerusalem, and a link to the airport. I had been warned to insist on a price before ever taking a taxi home. But that day, I walked home briskly in high spirits. As I approached Kfar Daniel, I quickened my pace. I entered my house with all my goodies. The children were excited, clamouring for treats. Norman was pleased with the tobacco and complimented me on my new blouse. My increasing physical fitness resulted in a strong sense of well-being. The growing competence of my Hebrew skills gave me a sense of accomplishment and freedom — another notch in my integration into this crazy unique country that I so dearly loved.

It was five weeks before the holiday of Shavuot. On secular settlements and in secular homes, Shavuot was a festival celebrated as a time of the barley harvest, a pastoral spring holiday. In religious places, it was marked as the time of the receiving of the Ten Commandments. Actually, Shavuot represented both concepts and was celebrated accordingly.

David loved going to the *gan*. The children had planted quick growing seeds and sprouts — beans, potatoes and beets — in small containers. These small plants would be brought along in their containers as the children marched in the Shavuot procession to the fields. The seedlings were beginning to sprout. When David saw the new sprouts, he was eager to see how the seeds had changed and, in the process, he uprooted half the plants in the *gan*. Esther was beside herself when she discovered the devastation. Outraged, she immediately sent David home! It was always hard to keep up with David's excessive energy and curiosity.

"David, how could you do such a thing?" I asked.

"I was investigating. I'm going to be a scientist. It was fun."

"You upset a lot of people. Even your friends are mad at you when they saw how you ruined their plants. And Esther is really mad at you."

"What should I do?"

"I think you'd better go and apologize."

David thought for a moment and then said uncertainly, "Uh, okay. Will you come with me?"

"Yes. We'll go together."

Reassured, David was eager to go. As we neared the *gan*, David reached out to hold my hand, obviously feeling uncomfortable. When he got inside the building, all heads turned to look at him.

Esther said, "David do you want to say something to your *chaverim* (friends)? "

"I'm sorry," said this little three-and-a-half-year-old in a soft plaintive voice. "I messed up your plants and I'm really sorry."

"Children, will you accept your friend David's apology?"

"Okay," they said, reluctantly.

Esther said solemnly, "David, it is forbidden to destroy living, growing things. The earth is very precious and we must love it and take care of it and all the things that grow on it."

And so, the incident was closed and David learned a valuable lesson. Four weeks later, I watched with pride as the children from the pre-school, dressed all in white with floral wreaths in their hair, singing about spring, holding their fledgling plants, marched to present them on the makeshift stage of bales of hay, at the edge of the fields. Then came the primary school children bearing baskets of tomatoes, lemons, pomegranates, and figs. Some carried cotton plants and sugar beets. Finally came the teens, each carrying around their shoulders either a young calf, a lamb or a kid goat. Adults followed, bearing sheaves of barley, wheat and *tarovet* (a mix of grains). We sang songs and listened to speeches. Tables had been set up with cheese blintzes, *shamenet* (sour cream), strawberries, and cheese cake. We ate, laughed and talked together. A good time was had by everyone. As the sun set, Norman and I and our two sleepy children quietly walked down the path toward our house, deeply contented. We were at home. We were living effortlessly and normally in Jewish time, within the Jewish calendar.

One July afternoon, while Yishai, Mahrie, Dorothy and Basil were visiting at tea-time, we heard a thunderous noise. Our settlement was right on the border of the Green Line, the old 1948 boundary demarcation. We immediately thought we might be under attack. Alarmed, we rushed to peer out the windows. The entire sky had darkened. Vast swarms of locusts filled the entire sky and descended onto our fields. Sounds like a roaring buzz saw penetrated the air. We were terrified. The more experienced couples knew what was happening. Norman and I were too astonished to be reflective. Twenty minutes later, the sky brightened as the locusts flew away.

Our entire crop of sugar beets, beans and potatoes was gone — devoured! It was total devastation.

"It's like living in biblical times!" I exclaimed. "This must have been how Pharaoh felt when the plague of locusts descended in ancient Egypt? Overwhelmed by the power of nature. Have we really advanced so little since those times?"

I couldn't believe that all our months of hard work and the promise of a bumper crop had disappeared in just 20 minutes. This was life in the Middle East. The swarm of locusts created an agricultural crisis for us. Fortunately, since it was still early in the summer, the agriculture committee decided it was possible to replant those lost crops. Members picked themselves up and grimly started all over again. They called a *giyoos* (mobilization) and every man, woman and teen on the *meshek* went down to the fields after 4:00 p.m. for three days and the following two *Shabbatot*, and helped to replant the sugar beets, potatoes and beans. It wasn't until several years later that pesticides and satellite imaging were used to control and prevent the proliferation of locust swarms.

It was August, and each day the sun grew hotter. We were experiencing the days of *chamsin*, the hot dry winds from the East. Some people experienced severe headaches. Others seemed to become more tense or anxious. Occasionally, tempers flared. We took longer siestas and tried to stay indoors as much as possible.

Eventually the eastern winds came less frequently and life returned to a more normal pattern.

I was a relatively courageous woman. I fancied myself as an adventurer. Hadn't I packed up everything that was near and dear to me and sailed with my adventurer husband and two young children to this challenging land? I accepted without complaint cooking on a primitive paraffin burner, living with the bare necessities of furnishings, a limited food supply, hot searing weather, unchallenging mind-numbing work, lizards, spiders, etc. But scorpions? Scorpions terrified me. They were too much!

It was after siesta. The children were still asleep and Norman had gone down to the fields. When I opened my front door to go to Dorothy's to borrow a cup of sugar, staring straight up at me sat a scorpion with its tail erect. Gasping for breath, I quickly shut the door. Frozen, and totally immobilized, I breathed deeply, vainly trying to calm down. What to do? I was in shock. My fear was palpable, so deep that I couldn't open the door even a crack to see if the scorpion had left. I sat there for nearly 40 minutes, until Norman returned. As he approached the house, I called out to him in a quavering voice from the other side of the door. "Norm, there's a scorpion at the door. I'm afraid to go out. Please, please do something."

Norman couldn't believe what he was hearing. It wasn't the presence of the scorpion that confounded him; it was the sheer terror in my voice. Norman set its tail afire and the scorpion immolated itself. As Norman held me trembling in his arms, he was amazed at the vulnerability of this intrepid wife of his. But even courageous wives have their limits.

CHAPTER 6

Individual Needs & Collective Imperatives

Hope is the thing with feathers that perches in the soul,
And sings the tunes without the words — and never stops at all.
— Emily Dickinson, "Hope"

A month later, the first of several *giyoosim* were called that fall. The cotton needed to be picked at its appointed time, and we did not have enough field workers. Every man, woman, and teen went down to the fields from 4 to 6:00 p.m. and picked cotton by hand. The *meshek* chose not to use a cotton-picking machine because it destroyed some of the fibres and left too much of the cotton in the boll. Chanan, our agricultural coordinator, organized and showed everyone how to cleanly pick the cotton from its boll.

After two strenuous hours, I was astonished to see how little I'd collected in my sack and how light it was. It took hours of backbreaking work to accumulate even one pound of cotton. It was truly stoop-crop work. I was sweating profusely, my arms ached, and my back was killing me. I gained a deeper and sincere respect for cotton pickers.

Norman and I loved the physicality of the land. We loved the dry hot sun with its merciless energizing white light, the harsh brown colours of this raw rocky bare land and the earthiness of life in sandals and shorts. The evenings were filled with low-hanging brilliant stars that lit up the night. In the dark blanket of silence, we could hear the lonely calls of the jackals. We felt a sense of total completeness, of wholeness.

I felt that I was a link to 2,000 years of history. The yearning for Eretz Israel had been a consistent theme that ran throughout our history. I recalled Yehuda Ha Levi's poem, written in Spain: "My heart is in the East, And I am in the uttermost West ..." And again in Psalm 137: "If I forget thee Oh Jerusalem, may my right hand lose her skill." I thought of Tisha B'Av, when we sing, "By the waters of Babylon, there we sat, and wept when we remembered Zion." I could feel all that historical yearning.

I connected with the guttural, nuanced ancient mystical language of Hebrew. I felt vital. My awareness of self as different — as Jewish — no longer encompassed me. I was just living it. Now it was as normal as breathing. Norman, a secularist, believed in the socialist communal aspects of the life and avidly followed the politics. When doubts arose, I comforted myself, reassured that this truly was our home.

The days rolled by. I watched with pride and delight as my two children became increasingly more Israeli, learning all the children's songs for each holiday, singing "Happy Birthday" in Hebrew, chanting children's Hebrew poetry. At night, I read to them from the children's poetry book, *Charuzim Adumim* (Red Beads). They were flourishing.

Tamar was becoming much less clingy. Little three-year-old Nomi Salant, who had befriended Tamar in the *gan*, soon became her best friend. They were inseparable.

Freddie Salant, Nomi's father, was the tractor mechanic on Kfar Daniel. When he realized Norman was a capable, proficient mechanic and tractor driver, he recommended that Norman be given that position. It seemed that Norman had paid his dues and had finally earned the opportunity of working at a permanent, more personally satisfying position.

Norman drove a Massey-Ferguson tractor. The children loved going to the edge of the hill to meet him and get a ride back. They knew the name of every tractor on the *meshek*: John Deere, Ford, and Massey-Ferguson. We were a farm family. I, Gloria, who had grown up in Brooklyn, New York, was now a part of a farm family!

Yael, Nomi's mother, was a heavy-set young woman, loud, fun loving, and outgoing. She always had a warm smile and spoke Hebrew with a very thick British accent. The words were Hebrew, but the vowels were definitely

Cockney English. Hearing Yael's exaggerated accent always made me giggle.

As I was no longer cleaning the outhouses, I found myself assigned to *ginot noy,* beautification of the landscape of the *meshek*. We lived in the Lod valley, in a microclimate that tended to be hotter and drier than much of the surrounding territory. Near the *gan* stood the *sifria* (library), surrounded by a large patch of dry, rocky, weed-ridden ground. The goal was to make a beautiful green lawn with shrubs on this wild, arid, forbidding soil.

Nachama was in charge of *ginat noy*. A tall, strapping, broad-shouldered, no-nonsense ideological woman, she had spent her teen years in Montreal in *Hashomer Hatsair*, an extreme left-wing movement. She prided herself on being a *chalutza,* a pioneer, and could pull up weeds with her bare, tough, callused hands.

Along came Dorothy and I to work under her. Dorothy, a former British school teacher, with her fair hair and fair skin, was an English rose. She wore a big floppy hat to shade her face and extra thick gardening gloves. I, a naïve student and young mother from North America, was eager to try new things and was a willing participant. I was provided with gardening gloves, in case I felt I might need them.

Every morning, we worked from nine to eleven o'clock. Dorothy saw only the futility of the exercise and grumbled for the entire two hours. "This is silly," she said. "Who needs a lawn up here? Nobody ever walks in this part of the *meshek*. Why don't we garden closer to where people are already living?" These remarks would be interspersed with, "The sun is broiling" or "Nobody should be outside in this heat" or "I'm sweltering." Occasionally, she would moan, "Even with gloves, my hands are killing me. Let's take a break."

Then Nachama would arrive and, in 10 minutes, pull up a huge patch of weeds, remove dozens of rocks, and tell us to put our shoulders to the wheel and push on. For four months, I watched the struggle and interplay between this English rose and the purist ideologue-pioneer, and wondered how people from such different backgrounds and values managed to find common cause, work and live together. This seemed to be the ultimate challenge of communal living.

Nachama's husband, Eliezer, was a tall angular man with bushy black hair and an equally bushy beard. He was the *nagar* (carpenter) and ran the carpentry shop, which was set up to produce furniture. It was supposed to bring in cash as our non-agricultural division. Eliezer loved to play with wood. He was very artistic. He carved the most beautiful candleholders, paperweights and Kiddush cups out of olive wood, but that did not make the carpentry shop profitable. The carpentry shop lost money every month and there was talk of closing it down.

The major question for the work committee was where to place Eliezer. He wasn't physically strong enough to work in the fields and the office was already over-staffed. So, he remained the *nagar* and the *meshek* continued to lose money. There was a constant tension in trying to create a balance between the diverse strengths, skills and inner resources of the individual members and the fundamental needs of the community.

Politically, it was a worrisome time. Every few days, another Israeli civilian was killed by Palestinian landmines or snipers, or in attacks from Syria. The newspapers were full of stories: a shepherd, a surveyor, a tractor driver, the wounded son of the Jerusalem mayor. It continued for months. Everyone was on edge. The country developed a kind of stoicism. When would it be our turn?

Conversely, there had also been many successes. Israel had completed the draining of the swamps in the Huleh valley, a major malaria breeding ground. The main concert hall, *Heichal HaTarbut*, in Tel Aviv, was built. The Olympic Committee of Israel was formed. Normalization with Germany was finally being implemented. El Al increased the size of its fleet of airplanes. People felt a sense of achievement and pride. They wavered between fear and stoicism. It was a difficult country to live in.

We were building a nation. We needed to people our land, to grow stronger. I dreamed of creating a just and compassionate Jewish society. I looked forward to each new immigrant as a building block in that society. In a week's time, Kfar Daniel would be receiving three new families from the Soviet Union. This was indeed historic because at that time, in 1958, it was extremely difficult for Russian Jews to emigrate from Russia. These families would arrive via Poland.

Alongside Sonia and Richard's house stood three empty houses ready to receive the Russian families. Everyone was excited. At last, the day arrived and Sasha and Tanya, Igor and Tamara, and Sergei and Lubliana were here. They knew very little about their Jewish heritage and often felt more Russian than Jewish. Whenever they mentioned anything Jewish, it generally referred to something a grandparent had said. Nevertheless, they were thrilled to be on Israeli soil. People on the *meshek* responded warmly, easing their integration into Israeli society.

Every evening, the men would go up to the *Bet Ha-Am* to find out their work assignment. Sonia's husband, Richard, the former Queen's Guardsman, had been given the Hebrew name, Reuven. In every way, Richard personified an Englishman. He was six feet, four inches tall and stood stiffly erect. Sonia had arrived in England from Nazi Germany on the *Kindertransport.* Before she left Germany, she had promised her parents that she would eventually settle in Israel. Although Richard had never met or interacted with a Jew before, he was smitten with Sonia at first sight. He said to himself, "I will one day marry her." As a couple, they both were snobbish, very proper and very selective about whom they befriended. They tended to keep to themselves. In many ways, the very British Richard was an anomaly on Kfar Daniel.

Igor and Tamara were their neighbours. When Igor would see Richard at the *Bet Ha-Am*, his warm out-going Slavic nature would take over. He would slap Richard on the back, greeting him effusively, shouting, "*Tovarich, Mah nishmah* (Comrade, How's it going)?" Richard would instantly stiffen, purse his lips and quietly respond, "Tov," and quickly move away. The irritation of conflicting cultures played itself out every evening. Igor was completely bewildered by British manners. It was a stand off. The open passionate warmth of social relationships among the Slavs was anathema to this stiff upper-lip Englishman.

However, communal life was fraught with much more profound complexities, sorrows as well as joys. Norman and I witnessed one such event, which challenged our very core values. There were two fundamental rules on all cooperative settlements. You could be immediately and summarily dismissed from the cooperative for violence — for example, for striking another *chaver* — or for stealing. There was no argument, no discussion; no compromise could be reached. These two basic tenets were well understood and accepted on all *kibbutzim* and *meshekim*.

Natan and Shoshana were an odd, socially isolated couple on Kfar Daniel. Natan was a self-effacing, thin, wiry individual who drove the truck that took the eggs from the *lul* (chicken coop) into Tnuva, the distribution cooperative for all the *kibbutzim*. Natan had grown up on a chicken farm in central New Jersey and came from a Habonim Labour Zionist background.

Shoshana, his wife, was thin and pale, with dark-brown stringy hair. Originally from Durban, South Africa, she also had a Habonim background. Shoshana's father was a renowned successful artist in South Africa. She, too, was an accomplished artist. Most of the women on Kfar Daniel tended to avoid her. Not one of them befriended her. They considered her a disorganized, untidy housekeeper. Because she salivated when she spoke, she seemed to be spitting when she talked. The couple had a one-and-a half-year-old daughter.

One day, Basil, our treasurer, discovered a discrepancy in the figures from *Tnuva* for the number of delivered eggs. It soon became apparent that Natan was selling a small number of eggs privately and keeping the cash. A meeting was held. Everyone attended. Evidence was presented. None of it was contested. A decision was made. Natan never said a word in his defense. He felt too humiliated. Shoshana never appeared. Kfar Daniel gave him two weeks to find another place and leave the *meshek*. It was a harsh, final decision and a tragedy. Natan and Shoshana were not bad people, just weak and inept. They had made a mistake. How would they manage? To see the sorrow and defeat in Natan's eyes touched me deeply.

I turned to Norman and said, "That was a Kangaroo Court! They didn't even try to find any mitigating circumstances. They were totally unforgiving. Where is

71

their humanity, their compassion?" Norman shook his head in disgust at the self-righteous mob rule we had just witnessed.

I was totally stricken to be part of the scene. I felt a deep sense of self-disgust that I had not stood up for my values and said something. Because I was intimidated to be the sole dissenting voice, I allowed myself to be part of a cruel, self-righteous process. Did I not have the courage of my convictions? Could I not stand up to a crowd even when mine was the only voice? These personal challenges troubled me deeply. How was I supposed to behave? It was indeed a trying time.

CHAPTER 7

A Potato Crop Failure

There was a time when meadow, grove, and stream,
The earth, and every common sight,
To me did seem
Apparelled in celestial light,
The glory and the freshness of a dream.
It is not now as it hath been of yore—
Turn wheresoe'er I may,
By night or day,
The things which I have seen I now can see no more.
— William Wordsworth, "Intimations of Immortality"

Nearly a year had come and gone. We were socially, physically and emotionally integrated into Kfar Daniel. David and Tamar were happy, inquisitive and self-confident at nearly four and three years old. They were our pride and joy. Our family was part of a very warm and supportive social group. We tended to discount the disquieting, disturbing moments that left us uneasy.

By the end of July, Norman was working mainly in potatoes. It promised to be a bumper crop. We were only 27 families and were in a financially precarious situation. Our potato crop would finally give us a solid financial footing. All hopes were focused on the sale of our potato crop. Norman was very optimistic. He took personal pride in the potato harvest and had invested his hopes and dreams in its success.

Mosheh, a *madrich chakla-oot* (roving agricultural instructor) assigned to our settlement, often came and had tea with us. He could tell the crudest jokes in Hebrew, which even made me blush. He told Norman that, although the potatoes looked good, they would have to be sprayed within a week or we could lose the entire crop.

Chanan was the *meshek's merakez chakla-oot* (coordinator of agriculture), and was responsible for overseeing the fields. Chanan's family had been prominent wealthy bankers in Germany. They put Chanan on the *Kindertransport* that carried thousands of Jewish children from continental Europe to England in the 1930s. As a result, he survived, while the rest of his family perished in the Holocaust. Chanan came to Israel in the late 1940s.

Five years earlier, there had been an opening at a two-year intensive course on agriculture. Because Chanan was one of the few bachelors on the *meshek*, he was the only one who could be spared. Consequently, he was designated to take the course and was subsequently made *merakez chakla'oot*. A charming bachelor, he preferred to spend much of his time up on the hill flirting with the women, married or single, than down in the fields. Unfortunately, he neglected to spray the potatoes and within weeks, they had all turned black with disease.

Norman was devastated and outraged. His anger and tension were palpable. He felt betrayed. How could anyone be so irresponsible! So many people's livelihoods depended on that potato crop. That loss finished it for Norman. He lost all faith in collective living. It was the death of a dream. "If I have to have a monkey on my back to live collectively, I'd rather go it on my own," he declared.

The *meshek's* financial situation worsened. It was a nightmare. All financial credit was suspended. We, the members, were now eating the emergency rations set aside in the event of war. Everything was rationed: tea, sugar, flour, etc. Members became dispirited. Norman grew quieter. He was grieving the loss of his dream. I tried to be supportive but a tension had been created in the household.

Sometimes comedy appears in the very midst of tragedy. I returned home from the *tsarchania* late one day after David and Tamar had already arrived from the *gan* and found the children busily mixing our entire month's rationed allotment of flour and sugar in a big bowl. The one small bottle of eau de cologne I had brought from Canada had been liberally poured into the mixture. The kitchen reeked. David looked up from his busy activities, smiled broadly and said, "We're making you a cake, *Ima.*"

I was beside myself. I sat down and began to cry. With all the recent stresses, this was too much to bear. Norman walked in and said, "Hey what's going on here? It smells like a Brussel's brothel."

"A Brussel's brothel!" I shouted angrily. "What do you know of a Brussel's brothel?"

As Norman surveyed the disarray, he began to see my distress. He encouraged the children to help clean up the mess. He set out to calm and reassure me and slowly order was restored.

In bed that night, I said to him, "Norm, what are we going to do? I didn't realize I'm under so much stress. I fly off the handle at any little thing. That is so not like me. Everyone is down because we are now *meshek moodrach*, under the complete control of the Jewish Agency. Everything is rationed. People have lost their spirit. And worst of all, it is hard to bear because we did it to ourselves! Nothing is fun anymore. You don't talk. I don't know what's going on with you. I'm so mixed up. I feel so lost." I began to cry.

"*Chabeebi*, don't cry. I'm sorry if I haven't been there for you. I'm trying to figure out what to do. I honestly don't know. I can tell you this. Seeing you this way just renews my desire to make a change. It's okay. We'll find a way. It will work itself out. Let's go to sleep. We've got to work tomorrow." We cuddled and fell sleep.

We were heading again into another winter. There seemed to be less socializing. The failure of the potato crop had dampened people's spirits and they became more inward. I knew life could not continue this way. Kfar Daniel was at a crossroads. Morale was very low. The issues were so painful that most members were reluctant to talk about them. Years later, I learned that Chanan became increasingly socially isolated and eventually left the *meshek*. Norman and I were also at a personal crossroads.

One day, I received a letter from an old friend, Darwin Eisen, a psychologist whom I had known at university in Vancouver. He and his family had made *aliyah,* immigrating to Israel two years earlier and were now living in Akko. He was the psychologist at the large 600-bed mental hospital there.

He had recently heard that my family and I were living in Kfar Daniel and wanted very much to make contact with us. I was delighted. He had been a married doctoral student when I was an undergrad. I remembered him as a bright, knowledgeable man with progressive values. We arranged for Darwin and family to visit on Shabbat. After the initial greetings, my first words were, "What's life like out there? Tell us what is happening outside of our cocoon."

Their very mature 10-year-old daughter, Belinda, decided to take charge of David and Tamar. They followed her around as if she were the Pied Piper. The adults sat around the table, drank tea, ate cookies, and talked.

Darwin and his wife, Sarita, described ancient Akko. "We love walking the streets of Akko," said Darwin. "It is full of alleyways and covered streets and hidden courtyards, and fantastic cafés and restaurants. We live in the new city, but I often shop at the *shuk* (market) in the old city, and I'm getting pretty good at bargaining. We spend many evenings just strolling about old Akko. The city has a 4,000-year-old history and has survived the Jewish, Greek and Roman periods. It survived the Crusades, the Mameluks, the Napoleonic invasion, the Ottomans, and now, of course, it is under Israeli control. It is a crazy and wonderful mix of Muslim and Christian Arabs, Bahais and Jews."

"I know," I said. "It has indeed a long history. I have such deeply cherished memories of Akko. We visited it a lot when we were together in Israel in 1950. Norm was hoping to have a boat built to sail around the world. It was quite an experience. In the end, we realized that Ali, the boat builder, only knew how to build boats without a keel that could only sail along the coast. They could not sail across oceans."

"Visiting us in Akko will actually be a kind of reunion for you, then," said Sarita. Darwin talked about his work at the hospital. Sarita worked as a nurse in a Kupat Cholim clinic. All four of us talked about how it felt to be a Jew in Israel, the good and the bad. We all talked about the tense political situation, the hostages and hostilities with Jordan.

I talked about living on a cooperative and how refreshing it was for me to talk about matters other than the *meshek*. Finally, I burst out, "Until your visit, I didn't realize how stifled I have been feeling. Don't get me wrong. I love my friends here. They are very good people. But I know what my neighbour is going to say before she even says it. And she knows how I will respond before I even open my mouth! I'm starving for some outside stimulation."

There was a long pause. Then Norman, looking directly at me, spoke slowly to Darwin. "I think I may have had it here. Do you think there might be some work for both of us near you?"

I paled. I was shocked. We had never discussed actually *leaving* Kfar Daniel. What had just happened? How was I to respond? I looked at Norman and realized that major changes were occurring that I hadn't really expected. What was going on? I said nothing.

"I understand," said Darwin. "Let me see what I can do."

Evening was beginning to fall and Darwin, Sarita and Belinda said their goodbyes. As we and the Eisens walked to our friends' car, Sarita said, "We'll keep in touch," and they drove away.

Later that night, we lay in bed not speaking. Finally, Norman broke the silence. "Gloria, I know I took you by surprise by what I said to Darwin. I've been thinking about this for some time. I've hesitated saying anything to you because I know how much the *meshek* means to you. You have such good friends here and feel so rooted. I was totally surprised by what you said about feeling so stifled. I hadn't realized that. I guess it gave me permission to honestly express myself. I didn't mean to hurt you."

"You blindsided me! It felt like it came from out of nowhere. I'm shocked and I'm angry, very, very angry! *Why didn't you tell me?* Why do I have to find out what you're thinking and feeling in the company of others? We have stopped talking. I felt your withdrawal but I couldn't put my finger on it. I need to know what you're thinking. I'm not a mind reader, you know. If you don't talk to me, I don't know what to do! You have to *tell* me!"

"Well, you have to tell me, too!" he exclaimed. "Why didn't you tell me you felt like you were stagnating?"

"Honestly, Norm, I didn't realize it myself until I began talking to Darwin."

"Okay. Speaking like that doesn't come easily to me. My automatic response is to clam up. I know we have to talk more. It's bloody hard. Perhaps it's a good lesson for both of us. I'll try."

"Good. Me, too. When you withdraw, I also withdraw. I feel so lonely. I need you. I'm scared, Norm. What are we going to do?"

"I don't know but I'm glad it's out now. Let's see if something develops from Darwin. If not, we'll have to put out some feelers. We can take our time and make sure we're making a sound decision."

"When you withdraw like that, I get so worried. I feel like I'm losing you. I love you so much. You're my very special man. I need you, Norm."

"And you have me, *Chabeebi.*"

We cuddled and slept soundly.

Life continued normally. Norman drove the tractor in the sugar beet field. I gardened with Dorothy. The children played, had their friends and thrived. But something was different. I began looking at our life through a new lens, a critical analytical lens. Would I ever be satisfied living in a tiny village? Was life as a farmer's wife fulfilling enough for me? What really were my ambitions? Consumed by my need to nurture and fulfill my Jewish identity, have I neglected attending to all my other fundamental personal needs? This was a wake-up call. I was pre-occupied and quieter, not my usual exuberant, enthusiastic self.

Dorothy noticed. "Gloria, something is different. What is going on? Do you want to tell me? I don't want to intrude. But if I can help ..."

"Please don't share this with anyone, Dorothy," I blurted. "I think *meshek* life might not be for us. Norm is unhappy and so am I."

"Did someone do or say something to upset you, Gloria?"

"No, it isn't that. People have been nothing but kind and generous to both of us. It is really a very good and kind *chevra.* I just think we may be more city than country people. Perhaps this lifestyle is not for us."

"What will you do? Where will you go?"

"We're kind of working that out now."

"Keep me in the loop, okay? I really care."

"I know. I care, too. I will, for sure."

Three weeks later, we received a letter from Darwin.

I read and reread the pertinent parts of the letter:

> For some time, we've been mulling over our future in this much loved but contradictory land and have finally decided to return to Canada. Too much Levantine red tape for me. The reasons are more complex and illogical than just that and too difficult to put in a letter. When we see each other face to face we can talk about it.
>
> About your request, I've looked into possible available positions. Gloria, an opening has occurred for a psychiatric social worker and I'm sure you could do it hands down. You will have to bring whatever documentation you have with you regarding your educational attainments. To contact the person in charge, write to Dr. Avram Cohen, Director of Social Services, Bet Cholim l'Çholei Ruach, Akko and arrange a meeting date. He is a reasonable man and a straight shooter.
>
> Norman, there is an opening for an occupational therapist at Mazra, a chronic care mental hospital, just down the road from Akko. No therapists have applied and I think they are desperate and will take totally unqualified people as long as you can handle a hammer, saw, and screwdriver. I'm not sure you will like it. But it may be a way to get you out of Kfar Daniel.
>
> I don't know what you will do for housing. But you can discuss that with Avram Cohen. He can be helpful.

Sorry I can't be of more help. See you when you come up to Akko. You know you can always stay with us. We have the room.

All the Best,
Darwin

As I read the letter, I paled. It was real. It might actually happen. Could I do it? Leave the *meshek*? Israel *was* Kfar Daniel. Leave my friends? How would the kids adjust? I was overwhelmed as I contemplated the change. I handed the letter to Norman. He read it and looked hard at me. His eyes softened with love and in a quiet voice said, "Shall we go for it?"

I smiled back. "But of course! What a question. 'Whither thou goest ...,' etc. Are we not intrepid adventurers? A new adventure?"

"Let's not say anything to the kids. We have already worked several *Shabbatot* (Sabbaths) to acquire some holiday time so we can travel to Akko without raising any eyebrows."

"I'll write to this Dr. Cohen and we'll set up a date, possibly in two or three weeks. What do you think?"

"That sounds about right. Let's give ourselves three full days and really make it a holiday."

"Yes. I'm beginning to feel excited. Norm, do you think it will be alright? Are we making the right decision? I mean, to leave the *meshek*? The kids are so integrated here. They're so happy."

"We'll just let things unfold."

Within weeks, plans were made and action was taken. Darwin met us at the bus station in Akko and drove us to his home in a suburb of Akko. We had an appointment with Dr. Avram Cohen the following day, a Friday afternoon, at two o'clock at the hospital. Belinda offered to look after David and Tamar.

I put on a navy skirt and my yellow floral blouse. Norman wore long pants and a shirt. We looked at each other and burst out laughing. "Will this be the new me?" we asked each other. Darwin drove us to our appointment with Dr. Cohen.

The Akko Mental Hospital was situated on the seaside, in the medieval walled city of Akko. I had read about its incredibly colourful history. It had been a Crusader fortress and consisted of many buildings within its compound. King Richard, the Lionhearted, had made Akko the capital of his Crusader kingdom after the fall of Jerusalem. Over those ruins, the Ottomans built a citadel. Napoleon tried to capture the citadel from the Ottomans and failed to penetrate the massive sea walls. During the British Mandate, it served as an army barracks, weapons warehouse and, later, an infamous prison, where they hanged three famous Jewish freedom fighters.

We approached the formidable 10-foot-high gate, gave our information to the guard and entered the grounds. Aware of its tumultuous history, we slowly walked to the stone administrative building. Dr. Cohen came out of his office to greet us and cordially ushered us into his office. He was an imposingly tall man in his mid-40s, who had come to Israel from Germany in his youth in the early 1930s.

He encouraged us to tell our story. As he listened to our narrative, he seemed warmed by our sincerity. He looked over my qualifications, noting that I had graduated with distinction as a Phi Beta Kappa. At the end of the interview, he offered both of us jobs, with a start date five weeks hence. He discussed our salaries and some housing possibilities. We left his office in a daze, stating that we would contact him within the next few days with our decision.

As we rode home on the bus, I felt anxious and ill at ease. When we turned the corner toward Kfar Daniel, a sense of familiarity overwhelmed me. We were coming home. How could I leave this place, which had become so dear to me?

As we walked down the path toward our home, David ran ahead, eager to see his friends, Amichai and Ephraim. It tore at my heart. Norman looked at me and said, "Don't say a word, Gloria." I nodded in agreement. We entered our house and silently made a light supper. The next morning, David and Tamar ran eagerly to the *gan;* Norman drove his tractor to the sugar beet field; I went to *ginat noy.* Nothing had changed, yet somehow everything had changed. We knew it. We felt it.

The next few days passed in a blur. I watched Norman functioning on automatic pilot. I knew that his heart was not in it. I knew that Dorothy and I were as close as sisters, but being wrapped up in the beguiling and comforting security of a family of friends was no longer enough for me. I watched my sturdy, self-confident, resilient children and was reassured that as long as we were together as a family, the children would continue to flourish.

Finally, I turned to Norman and said, "I guess the decision has made itself, hasn't it, Norm?"

"I've just been waiting for you to agree."

"Okay. I'll call Dr. Cohen first thing tomorrow morning."

Telling our inner circle was the hardest thing I had ever done. I felt as if I had betrayed them. As expected, many members stopped speaking to us. Our friends, however, continued to be supportive.

The wheels had been put in motion. I received a letter from Dr. Cohen stating that I was to start work at the hospital as a psychiatric social worker in three weeks from the date of the letter. Darwin and Shulamit, a social worker, would initially supervise me. Norman would start work at Mazra Hospital for the chronically mentally ill as an occupational therapist in four weeks. He would have a professional occupational therapist mentoring him. Basically, he only needed to be able to work some of the woodworking equipment. Norman would receive a monthly salary of 750 lira for full-time work. I would receive 500 lira for half-time work. Together, the money was more than ample. We could also rent cheaply a minimally but adequately furnished apartment within the gates of the hospital. There were some suggestions regarding a pre-school for the children.

I was shaken to my core. Although I knew we were making the right decision, my heart was torn. The children were acting up. They did not want to leave their happy home and could not understand why we were leaving. Frankly, I did not have any good answers either. Norman tried to be supportive. But once the decision had been made, he was most eager to leave.

Finally, the dreaded day arrived. We were all packed. Darwin arrived and we loaded his car as quickly as possible. David shouted and screamed, "*I'm not going!*" Norman lifted him up and seated him in the car with a stern warning not to move. David sat there bellowing and crying loudly. Tamar clung to me. Norman got in the car, stone-faced and we drove away. We felt horrible.

Sarita and Belinda were waiting for us at the hospital apartment in Akko. With everyone helping, we unloaded quickly. Sarita had brought a complete dinner. Belinda was remarkable with the children, especially David. She turned the exploration of the three-room apartment into a great adventure. Before long, David and Tamar were laughing and playing hide-'n-go-seek. Equanimity was restored.

The door to the apartment was nine feet high. In days gone by, perhaps a soldier had entered on horseback. The entrance led directly into a small kitchenette and dining area with a square table and four chairs. In a far corner was the door to the toilet, sink and shower. The room adjacent was a kind of sitting room/bedroom for the children, with minimal furniture, and off to the side were two smaller normal size doors that led to a large room with a double bed on an iron frame and no other furniture. The only window in the entire apartment was in that bedroom. The best that could be said about the apartment was that it was cheap and functional. The apartment was located around the corner from the cafeteria, where we would eat most of our meals.

Darwin, Sarita and Belinda stayed for a while and finally left, saying, "We'll pop around tomorrow shortly after noon. You need some time to adjust. It's a huge transition. Catch your breath. Remember, you are not alone. We want to help." Norman and I thanked them profusely as they said their goodbyes.

It was time to make up the children's beds and put them to sleep. I read David his favourite *Charuzim Adumim* and Norman read Tamar *Blueberries for Sal.* After warm kisses and hugs, we left our children and went into our bedroom. As we made up our double bed, Norman said, "Will you forgive me for causing you all this pain, Gloria?"

"I don't blame you, Norm. It's just a lot harder than I thought. I had such dreams about how I would live in Israel. I wanted to be part of building the country. I felt that in Kfar Daniel I was doing something worthwhile.

There was so much I loved about living on the *meshek*. It's just so hard to give up the dream." I began to cry.

"Ah, *Chabeebi*, life just isn't like that. I hoped that I would find in Kfar Daniel a sense of purpose and meaning in my life. Instead, I found a lot of small-minded, petty, mean-spirited people."

"You never said anything about that!"

"You and the kids seemed so happy and I thought I was just being cranky and hyper-critical."

"Norm, you've got to let me know how you are feeling. My goodness, here I am feeling so very sorry for myself. We're both grieving for the loss of our dreams. What is it I heard you say the other day to Darwin? 'Perhaps, I, too, came to kiss an old dream goodbye.' But it's still very hard to accept. We'll be okay. It will just take me a little longer to adjust. Norm, I want us to be happy, to be in sync. I just need a little time."

"Okay. Even though I don't often show it, just know that I'm here for you. Now, let's get some sleep. Tomorrow will be a better day." So ended our first day in Akko.

CHAPTER 8

New Beginnings

An Arab shepherd is searching for his goat on Mount Zion
And on the opposite hill I am searching for my little boy.
An Arab shepherd and a Jewish father
Both in their temporary failure.
Our two voices met above
The Sultan's Pool in the valley between us.
Neither of us wants the boy or the goat
To get caught in the wheels
Of the "Had Gadya" machine.
Afterward we found them among the bushes,
And our voices came back inside us
Laughing and crying.
Searching for a goat or a child has always been
The beginning of a new religion in these mountains.
— Yehuda Amichai, "An Arab Shepherd is Searching
for his Goat on Mount Zion"

At 7:00 a.m., David and Tamar burst into our bedroom, full of energy and curiosity about their new home. "*Abba, Ima*, what are we doing today? Are we going to visit someone new? Where are the new friends you said we would find here?"

"David, today we'll explore a new *gan*. Would you like that? In the meantime, let's get washed and dressed and then we can go to the cafeteria next door and have some breakfast."

We all walked together into the cafeteria, introduced ourselves to the supervising manager, and set up a system for payment. We selected our food and carried it around the corner to our apartment to eat as a family.

I had set up an appointment to meet Ruth, the *ganenet*, at the WIZO *gan* at 11:00 a.m. Norman had arranged to meet Darwin to tour Mazra. Slowly, I strolled down the main street in Akko with David and Tamar. The main street consisted of an extra wide paved road with stores on each side. There were several cafés and restaurants, two grocery stores, a small kiosk selling ice cream, several clothing stores, two shoe stores, a hardware store, a dry goods store, a Bank Hapoalim, a Bank Leumi, and a cinema. Eventually, we came to the turn-off to the *gan*.

We came upon a broad dark green building within a large fenced-in yard. The *ganenet* came out to greet us. She was a tall, angular woman, with a weather-beaten face and straight short salt-and-pepper hair. Her voice was deep and resonant. "*Shalom David v'Tamar. Korim li Root.*" (Hello. David and Tamar. My name is Ruth.)

"*Shalom Root,*" the children replied. Ruth quickly called over a few children and introduced them, and within minutes the children had run off to play.

I entered the *gan* and Ruth showed me around. It resembled a daycare more than a pre-school. There were small sinks and hooks for each child's towel and places where the children kept their toothbrushes. Each child had a cubby for stowing their gumboots or shoes and hooks for their outerwear. Near the kitchen was an array of small tables and chairs. Depending on how much time they spent at the pre-school, some children ate all three meals there. There was a large room for arts and crafts, music and dance, a dress-up corner, and sundry toys. They had a storage area for the mats used for rest period, and ample showers and toilets. An unusual and creative outdoors playground filled with a variety of discarded item and imaginative junk surrounded the building, including the remains of an old car embedded in the ground.

Ruth explained that many of the children were the offspring of new immigrants, often from Arab countries. Many children stayed there all day. The *gan*'s goal was to teach the children good hygiene and positive habits. They fostered creative play, inquisitiveness, problem solving, and self-worth, in an atmosphere of security and safety. My children seemed to take to the *gan* seamlessly.

I was impressed with their understanding and comprehensive care and felt heartened by Ruth's warmth, intelligence and sensitivity. We agreed that I would bring David and Tamar there beginning the next morning at eight o'clock and pick them up every day at 1:00 p.m., thus enabling me to work from 8:30 to 12:30.

After lunch and siesta, Darwin and Sarita invited us over for four o'clock tea and greeted us warmly. "How are you settling in?" asked Darwin.

"Not too badly," replied Norman. "Mazra feels a bit weird to me, but I suppose it's a job and I'll get used to it. The staff seem pleasant. We have to give it time."

I chimed in. "I took the kids to the *gan* this morning and the *ganenet* was really very impressive — smart, compassionate, intuitive, with lots of experience and skills."

"If there is one thing the Israelis do well, it is their early childhood development," said Darwin. "They've studied the Scandinavian systems and put their money and training into their youth. For them, everything is geared to their future, and that is their youth. It's when they get a bit older that I worry. Elementary school is adequate. But secondary school is very old style, European-lecture style, authoritarian, top down, and expensive."

"What do you mean, Darwin?" I asked.

"It's hard to explain. I'm working with the senior people at the hospital, who are from Romania. I find a kind of hidden deference to status, class, and authority. They're the intelligentsia, but they're pretty rigid. As a Canadian, I was raised in a pluralistic, pragmatic society. Mind you, there are many wonderful people here and I love being in a Jewish land. Belinda has thrived here. She is our pride and joy. Some of the boorish aggressive behaviour we see encouraged in children is worrisome. Sarita and I don't feel at home here, intellectually or culturally."

"I think I understand where you're coming from," said Norman.

Startled, I said, "Wow, you've given us a lot to think about."

The conversation drifted to personalities, doings in Akko, Israeli politics, and general chitchat. On the way home, I asked Norman, "Do you feel like Darwin, Norm?"

"I don't know, *Chabcchi.*"

The next morning Norman hopped the bus at 7:30 for Mazra. I washed and dressed the children and walked them to the *gan* and then went to the hospital to meet with Shulamit, the social worker. A routine was emerging.

Shulamit, 42, was a medium-height, plump *sabra* with a round face surrounded by a profusion of golden curly locks. When she smiled, her entire face lit up. She vibrated warmth and caring. She spoke English perfectly, with an Israeli accent.

"Galila, yes? I'm Shulamit. It's so good to meet you. Would you like some coffee or tea?"

"I would love some tea."

Shulamit put on her electric kettle, laid out all the necessities, and talked the entire time. "I lived in Haifa most of my life. I was a social worker there. I lost my husband in the Suez campaign in 1956. We were married 18 years, no children. So, I moved to Akko and got this job in the hospital. End of story. So, tell me something about yourself. Why did you leave Kfar Daniel?"

"Honestly, I'm not sure why we left. It was a huge uprooting for me and the kids. I think I needed a broader landscape and more challenge. I loved Kfar Daniel and my kids were thriving but there was a sameness there and I was hungry for more stimulation. I guess I needed more diverse challenges, something that would stretch me."

We talked and talked — about my friendships on Kfar Daniel, my life in Canada and my family in the United States. Shulamit was easy to talk to and an attentive listener.

"Galila, you have a wonderful outlook on life. I can see that you are very open to new experiences. I think we'll get along famously. You and I will share this office. When you're interviewing, we have another room. Let's go to the wards and I'll show you around."

So began my introduction to the Akko Mental Hospital, otherwise known as *Bet Cholim L'Cholei Ruach,* the hospital for the sick in spirit. Finally, it was time for me to pick up the children at the *gan.* I walked briskly along the main thoroughfare of Akko. It was an early winter day with a cold nip in the air. The fine cool breeze energized me. I was beginning to feel more reconciled to meeting the new challenges in my life.

At the *gan,* David and Tamar greeted me enthusiastically. "They have a lot of toys here," David said. "Everybody shares. I drove the car that is outside. It was fun."

Tamar was more noncommittal. "It's okay. I haven't found a best friend yet. But they seem nice."

The children and I slowly walked home. We went to the hospital cafeteria for our mid-day dinner and then settled down for siesta. Shortly thereafter, Norman joined us. After siesta, I got up, looked at Norman, who was lying in bed awake looking troubled.

"What is it, Norm? What's the matter?"

"I don't know if I can do this."

"What do you mean?"

"Dealing with sick disabled people just isn't my thing. I feel terrible there. I'll stick with it in the meantime. But I need to find something else."

I was silent. I knew Norman would not say anything more but his situation was worrisome. However, I clung to the belief that somehow Norman would find an answer.

The days rolled by. The children rushed eagerly to the *gan*. I thoroughly enjoyed working with Shulamit. The work was new to me. I was learning new things all the time. I thrived on all the new challenges. I was taking in-depth case histories from relatives of patients, which I was able to do in Hebrew and then write up in English.

When Darwin read one of my case histories, he laughed, saying, "When you translate from the Hebrew, your English is very stilted, as if English is not your first language."

Meanwhile, I could see that Norman was becoming increasingly quiet. I worried about what might be going on.

One afternoon, Norman said, "Why don't we go into the old city and see if we can find Mustafa Shami?"

"I think that's a fabulous idea." I recalled those heady times in 1950 when Norman and two South African adventurer friends had intended to sail around the world. They negotiated with an old Arab boat builder, Ali. Norman often brought me, his new girlfriend, along to these negotiations. Mustafa was one of the interpreters. I soon became friends with Mustafa's wife, Subhia.

Now, in 1959, Norman and I, David and Tamar walked past the huge dry moat that surrounded the walled old city to the city's large open gate. We walked through the main thoroughfare, Market Street. The winding narrow covered streets, unexpected courtyards, and the familiar combined odour of cardamom, garlic, cumin and urine filled our senses. Eventually, we came to a central square of artisans, boat builders, cabinetmakers, and a blacksmith.

Norman spotted Mustafa working at his forge. Of medium height, with light olive skin, green eyes, and short light brown hair, Mustafa was still lean and wiry. Norman shouted, "Mustafa!" Mustafa looked up perplexed. Suddenly recognizing Norman, he threw down his tools, and ran toward him. With a big smile, he threw his arms around Norman and they hugged one another. They hadn't seen each other in eight years, but it felt as if it were just yesterday! Smiling broadly, they began to reminisce.

"Do you remember the young girl I always brought with me, Mustafa? I married her. And here she is with our two children."

"Subhia said that girl would be the one. You have beautiful children. Come my friend, sit. We will have coffee and later, we go to my house." Mustafa sent his oldest boy, Jihad, to bring us coffee. He sent his son, Achmed, ahead to tell Subhia to prepare for us later.

Suddenly, a young man came across the square and embraced Norman. "You do not remember me? I am Mohamed, Ali's son. You took out a piece of glass from the bottom of my foot. I never forgot such a kindness from a stranger. Do you remember?"

"Of course. You were 14 or 15. How are you? How is your father?"

"My father died last year and only my father's second wife still lives. My brother and I run the boat building business now. We use all modern electronic equipment and make patrol boats for the Israeli government. We have much work. Life is good."

They embraced and Norman said, "Stay well my friend. I'm happy to see you again."

After Mohammed left, Mustafa continued. "Mohammed and his brother are the younger generation, with power tools and all. They do very well." Mustafa invited us to his house. We walked together through tunneled streets and finally a side street appeared. There were the familiar steps along the side of a wall that took us into Mustafa's house. Subhia greeted me and the children warmly and lovingly. She immediately served us coffee in small cups without handles — sweet, hot, and spiced with cardamom. We talked about our families, our children, our brothers, our sisters, etc. We talked for hours, catching up on their lives. It felt like coming home.

"Mustafa, how is it for you living under Israeli rule?" asked Norman.

"For me, it is always the same. First, we had Turkish rule, but mostly they left us alone. Then, we had British rule. They also left us alone. The Israelis make more rules, but mostly I work around them."

"What do you mean?" I asked. "How can you work around them?"

"Well, for example, we are only allowed to have a two-inch pipe bringing water into our house. But with the two-inch pipe, there is no pressure and the water just trickles in. So, I put in a three-inch pipe, which works very well. But when the Israeli inspector came to check, I switched it to the two-inch pipe. As soon as he left, of course I switched the pipe back to the three-inch one. We just work around restrictions."

We all laughed and continued eating and drinking coffee. It was a wonderful reunion. Mustafa insisted we come again the next evening so we could all go to the Abu Christo restaurant. We agreed.

As we walked home, Norman said, "Seeing Mustafa somehow makes living here more meaningful."

"I'm so glad, Norm. I do want you to be happy." I finally felt a sense of relief from the anxiety I was carrying about him.

The following evening, we wandered back to Mustafa and Subhia's house. We bedded Tamar and David there, with their daughter, Arabia, acting as baby-sitter and the four of us strolled to the Abu Christo restaurant. The table was soon covered with seven or eight salads, shredded sweet-and-sour carrots, tomatoes and cucumbers, greens, lentils, chickpeas, tabouli, a variety of eggplant salads and fish platters. The pastries were very sweet, many of them dripping with honey.

We talked about the Arab-Israeli situation. Mustafa was concerned for the safety of his older brother, Mohammed, who had actively opposed Israeli control. "I held a gun to his head and told him, 'You and your family have to leave now. You have to go to Lebanon, where we have close relatives. It is too dangerous for you here.'" Mustafa missed them because they had been very close. Mohammed was married to Subhia's sister.

However, they visited Lebanon often and had been to all their nieces' weddings. The borders were porous. Many of Akko's inhabitants were fishermen and sailed back and forth to Lebanon. Cardamom did not grow in Israel, only in Lebanon. Yet, most Israeli Arabs openly drank their coffee spiced with Lebanese cardamom.

"Mustafa, would you want to join Mohammed in Lebanon?" Norman asked.

"No, I live better here."

Soon, we were seeing Mustafa and his family on a daily basis. In addition to their two oldest children whom we had met in 1950, there were now five more, for a total of eight. Arabia was actually being raised by Subhia's older sister. Achmed was the child she was carrying when we had left. Since then, Radah, Anya, Nadia and Saleh had been born.

David, at four, was close to Saleh's age and they became inseparable. Saleh was as mischievous as David. One day I walked into Subhia's house and found Saleh and David, stripped naked, being scrubbed with a luffah by Subhia. They had gotten themselves into a pile of black dirt. Subhia made no skin-colour distinctions — black, white, or anything in between. A child was a child and she loved them all.

Nevertheless, Arabs made their own sharp distinctions between shades of skin colour. Mustafa and Subhia were clearly light-skinned and Mustafa was green-eyed. When Norman and I attended a Moslem wedding in Akko, where the bride's parents were from the Sudan, we overheard many derogatory comments made about the dark-skinned Sudanese bride. There was an unacknowledged pecking order based on shades of skin colour. This prejudice seemed to be almost universal.

CHAPTER 9

Challenges & Frustrations

There are a thousand ways to kneel and kiss the ground;
There are a thousand ways to go home again.
— Rumi, *Famous Quotes*

We visited Darwin and his family for the last time. "Going back is hard," he told us. "It's easy to love this country. It's so vibrant, so exciting, people are so alive and committed. It's wonderful to be part of this country. But I worry about Belinda. The educational system does not fit with our philosophy and the higher you go, the more expensive and authoritarian it becomes. Also, the youth are raised to be more aggressive, loud, and at times they are even boorish. I just don't like the attitude it breeds of superiority and boastfulness. I feel conflicted. It hurts but I feel we have to leave."

We could sense his ambivalence. I wondered, *Will I start to feel similar feelings? Will I too begin to feel estranged?* It frightened me. "You've been very kind to us and I hate to see you leave. But I understand. Stay in touch."

"We will."

With tears in our eyes, we hugged and said goodbye. It was a major loss. They had been such good friends. Now we were truly on our own.

I looked at Norman and said, "Will we become like the Eisens, Norm? I am afraid. I really want to find a way to be part of this country. It means so much to me."

"I know, *Chabeebi.* We'll give it our best shot. But I need to find another job, that's for sure."

One day, Norman came home, crouched over and hobbling. He had slipped a disc and dislocated his back. He could barely walk. He was immobilized in bed for three full days.

As his mobility gradually returned, he said, "Gloria, I can't go back to Mazra. I can't work in a place where a person has been nailing the same piece of wood over and over again for the past 10 years. They are chronically mentally ill and have not progressed for many years. We are only maintaining them. It is deadening work and it is making me ill."

"I understand, Norm. Frankly, I would feel the same way. It's enough to make you feel crazy yourself."

"I heard of a possible opening at a branch of the Kaduri School on the road to Mazra. I need to look into it. As soon as I can get around, I'll go check it out."

"What is Kaduri?"

"Kaduri is a very famous scholarly, exclusive agricultural high school and junior college. Some of the most famous kibbutz elite — General Yitzchak Rabin, the poet, Chaim Guri, and the famous archeologist, General

Yigal Allon, who was one of my commanding officers in the Israeli War of Independence — attended Kaduri. It's very well known in this country. Its main location is near Afulah but there is a branch just up the road near Mazra. A guy at work told me they are looking for a *madrich* (counselor) to monitor and guide their students socially. I think it might work for me. Kibbutz youth are quite inspiring."

"Norm, what a perfect fit. It sounds very promising. Go for it!"

Several days later, Norman returned home with a big grin on his face. He was buoyant. He would start his new job at Kaduri as a *madrich*, a mix of counselor, social leader and guide, on the following Sunday. He had great intuitive people skills and I knew he would do well there. Once again, we were a contented family, and all on the same page.

Several weeks later, Norman invited Chaim, one of Kaduri's English teachers, to our apartment for dinner. Chaim, a charming man in his early 30s, spoke fluent Arabic and had also been a scholar of Arabic history and culture. He talked about the golden period in Arab history, from about 750 to 1250 A.D. The two of us listened, fascinated, with rapt attention.

"The word *algebra* is derived from the Arabic *al-jabr*, meaning restoration. Although Arabic numerals were invented in India, they were introduced to the West by the Arabs. They understood how numbers defined the world. They invented the zero. Imagine how limited the world was without the concept of the zero! What a profound concept that was, and how it opened up so many new possibilities."

"That's amazing," I said. "I had no idea."

"The sciences of astronomy and mathematics, in particular, flourished during this period. They also developed geometry, trigonometry, calculus, and algorithms."

"I had heard that they were quite advanced in medicine, too." said Norman.

"There was enormous progress in medicine," Chaim continued. "In the city of Baghdad, alone, there were 860 licensed physicians. Imagine! In 956 A.D., the Christian King of Leon was cured by the Moorish physicians of Cordoba. There were notable individual physicians, in the tenth and eleventh centuries. Our own sage and physician, Rambam (Maimonides), learned from them. Al-Razi wrote a book on smallpox and Ibn-Sina of Bukhara, was known in the West as the famous Avicenna. He wrote the *Canon of Medicine* that was later translated into Latin and dominated European medical studies for centuries."

"Yes, I've heard of them but didn't really realize their significance," said Norman.

"Certainly, the Arabs were far more advanced than their contemporary Europeans. Medical facilities traditionally closed every night, but by the tenth century, laws were passed to keep hospitals open 24 hours a day, and hospitals were forbidden to turn away patients unable to pay. Eventually, charitable foundations were formed to support hospitals, as well as schools. This money supported free medical care for all citizens."

"It really goes to show how socially minded people were even in those days," I said. "And what an advanced sense of social justice they had for those times! Why aren't we taught this in school? Our relationship with the Arabs would be so different."

Chaim replied, "Many civilizations became great and eventually waned. Look at Greece and Rome. We took the good from the Arabs, built upon it, but due to ignorance of their greatness, do not admire them. We owe them a lot."

Norman, ever the researcher and bookworm, added, "How right you are. I need to read up on all this. What books would you recommend to get me started?"

The conversation continued until well into the night. As we lingered over our goodbyes, we each said how much we enjoyed the evening and promised to do it again.

When Chaim left, Norm turned to me. "I told you, Gloria, they have some very smart people at that school."

Norman was touched by the idealism of the youth at Kaduri. "This morning, I monitored the kids when they took their final exams. They really have a genuine honour system. They received their exam papers and then scattered individually all over the lawn and sat down to write them. No one talked. No one looked at the other. Each one was preoccupied with his own paper.

I've never seen anything like this. You know, they can raid the fridge at midnight and I have to admonish them because the cook is furious. But when it comes to their studies, they are totally serious, committed and honourable."

"That's inspiring. It's good to think that many of them will probably become our future leaders. I hate to think that they automatically go into the army when they finish at Kaduri."

"That is the ultimate reality of our life here, Gloria."

"Don't I know it," I replied, thinking of our David.

As the days went by, I became more engaged in my work. I found it both interesting and challenging. I attended the weekly rounds with the hospital's chief medical officer, Dr. Matescu, a Jewish psychiatrist from Romania. He seemed to know only one way to deal with patients. Each week, he would recommend either reducing or increasing their medication. But nothing more. That seemed to be the formula for almost all care: raise or lower the dosage. This limited perspective made me shake my head in dismay.

I observed shock treatment. As I watched a patient's body convulse and face contort, I turned to Shulamit and said, "This seems so inhumane. I can't believe we think this treatment is beneficial."

"But we do see results, Galila. The depression is greatly reduced."

"Yes, but at what cost? They lose much of their memory."

"But Dr. Matescu is well trained and knows more than we do. He is the authority."

"I don't know. I grew up in the States and we usually question everything, especially authority."

And so it went. I often met the next of kin, took case histories, and counseled family members. One day, I said to Shulamit, "I interviewed the husband of an Arab-Israeli. He is a 56-year-old fisherman, and she is 26. He married her when she was 14. She recently connected with a young Arab man and was secretly meeting him. When her husband heard of this, he beat her and stopped the liaison. She cut out a picture of a stallion and pinned it on the front door of the house. She believed the spirit of the horse would send a message to her lover to come back to her. She is diagnosed as paranoid schizophrenic.

"The husband told me that he loved his wife very much since he had taken her as a young girl and raised her to adulthood. He had mentored and guided her. I asked him if he ever beat her. He replied, 'Only when she disobeyed and needed it.' He felt he was both husband and father. This seems to me so much more like an ethno-cultural issue than a psychiatric one and should be dealt with in that context. Don't you agree, Shulamit?"

"I do. But we don't have a mandate to do that. Perhaps if that man had gone to see one of the more enlightened imams, or some leader within his community, they might have found another way than our highly medicalized institution. But this is not my job." Shulamit shrugged and turned away.

I was disappointed but accepted her position. She continued to be a source of information, a support and a good friend to me.

I also administered several psychological tests. It struck me as ironic when testing a young Jew from Morocco, to find that he was fluent in four languages but had an IQ of only 87. Clearly, he was a low-functioning linguist. He knew French, Arabic, Hebrew, and English, but only at a limited functional level. I thought this put the lie to the prevalent European snobbism that knowledge of many languages was a sign of high intellect and culture.

Male and female patients were housed separately and all their activities were gender-segregated. Only on Friday evenings, when a film was shown on the lawn, were both genders present, divided by a mesh wire fence. Nevertheless, a small minority of women always seemed to get pregnant on those occasions. I scratched my head in amazement that people could be so driven to express their sexual urges, and perhaps procreation needs, that they were able to find a most unlikely way. So much for gender segregation!

One of my patients was a 29-year-old woman who never uttered a word. Her story was tragic. She was an only child living with her parents in Germany in 1940. At the age of 10, they went into hiding. During that time, she was told not to make a sound. Just before the end of the war, her parents were discovered and shot. Miraculously, she survived and made her way to Israel. She had been in Akko Mental Hospital since her arrival in 1950. I tried speaking to her gently. She would make eye contact but could not verbally respond. She represented an overt living tragedy of the Holocaust.

People shared each other's joys and sorrows. We were both a nation state and also a family. This often led to a kind of instant ersatz intimacy, with all its pros and cons. The 1950s were still a time of strong nationalism in Israel.

One day, for example, while I was walking down the street with the children, David began to act up and simply would not heed my frustrated warnings. Exasperated, I shouted harshly to him in English. A woman approached and admonished me. *"Rak Ivrit, Gveret. Rak Ivrit"* (only Hebrew, only Hebrew, Madam). The implied message was: We were building a nation united by one national language and I should know that! She felt she had a right and a duty to rebuke me.

The prevailing sense that all of us, Jews, were one family also permitted people to ask strangers the most personal questions. Riding on a bus or sitting beside a total stranger, you might be asked, "How much money do you earn? What do your parents do? What are your ambitions? Do you have a husband or a boyfriend?" After all, we are all Jews, all one family, are we not?

One day, while bringing both children home from the *gan*, David insisted on getting an ice cream along the way. He stood in the middle of the sidewalk, shouting and screaming in the blazing heat of the noonday sun. Totally frustrated and at my wit's end, I turned him around and smacked his bottom. Immediately, a woman came up to me and sternly said, "*Lo l'harbits, lo l'harbits*" (do not hit, do not hit). She felt it was her responsibility to correct me. After all, we are one big family! Are we not?

How I longed for a bit of anonymity in this connected, one-family world. A part of me longed for the privacy to do as I liked, not to have to answer to others, especially strangers. These feelings were always there underneath the surface. Nevertheless, Israelis felt engrossed in their common struggle to build a state and I could feel this reassuring warmth of one family. It was the reverse side of that coin.

As the weeks and months rolled by, we spent a great deal of time in the old city with Mustafa and his family. I decided to reciprocate their hospitality by inviting Mustafa and Subhia to a traditional Friday night *Shabbat* meal of chicken soup with *kneidlach* (matzah balls), roast chicken, potatoes, green beans and a tomato-cucumber salad, followed by sponge cake and tea for dessert. I worked all day preparing the food and was very proud to host them.

They entered the apartment full of smiles and warmth. As Norman and I began to serve the dishes, the atmosphere changed. They barely touched the food. The meal was a disaster! They simply could not eat the food.

Without any of their seasonings, it all was tasteless to them, like eating straw. They were polite and simply said they were not very hungry. They didn't even like the challah! I didn't know what to do. It was indeed a humbling experience.

One day, while Norman and I were visiting Mustafa at his blacksmith shop, we experienced an excruciating moment. Rada and Saleh, who had been playing with our children, ran in, shouting that they couldn't find David and Tamar. Norman and I were shaken to our core. David and Tamar had disappeared? I couldn't believe it. All children in old Akko were safe, weren't they? Everyone loved children, didn't they?

There were courtyards within courtyards, apartments within apartments. Mustafa immediately set out to search for them. I watched Mustafa carefully and could tell that he was worried. We were now in his hands. He and his family had lived in Akko for many generations. He knew Akko and its people intimately.

He sent me to his house to wait with Subhia. He sent his two older sons, Jihad and Muchmud, to neighbouring houses to inquire. Norman and Mustafa searched several houses. After nearly two hours of unbearable anguish, they found the two children, safe and unharmed.

There was a woman who had had several miscarriages and was desperate for a child. Everyone in the town knew her. She had enticed the children with sweets and then locked them in. Mustafa approached her slowly and carefully, and persuaded her to unlock and open her door. David and Tamar rushed to Mustafa's side. He gently thanked the sobbing woman and took the children home. When David and Tamar entered the Shami household, I burst into tears, hugging and kissing them.

CHAPTER 10

Contradictions, Confusion

Tell all the truth but tell it slant —
Success in Circuit lies
Too bright for our firm Delight
The Truth's superb surprise
— Emily Dickinson, "Tell all the truth but tell it slant"

Norman enjoyed his work at Kaduri. He had developed an amicable and respectful relationship with the students and faculty. However, he could not see a career path through this work. Where would he go? What could he do? Was this the most meaningful work he could aspire to? He was constantly aware of his limitations in this country, but he was torn between his feelings and his awareness of how deeply attached his wife and children were to this land.

For Norman, the bright light in his day was time spent with Mustafa. One day, Mustafa was commissioned by a wealthy sheik to create a special filigreed wrought iron cradle for his first-born son. It consisted of lacy ironwork, scrolls and arabesques. As I gazed upon this work of art, I was awed. "Mustafa, this is absolutely exquisite. You must do more of this. If you want, I would be happy to sell it for you. You could make a fortune." I was overwhelmed by his craftsmanship and artistic expression.

Mustafa smiled at me and calmly said, "It was too much work and I couldn't wait to finish it. I broke my bellows to get some rest. I won't be able to work now for a week. Come, let's go for a walk and have some fun." A reminder that this was a different culture with different values.

While visiting Mustafa at work, Norman and I met Earl McCoy, a volunteer with the American Friends Service Committee of the Quaker Society. He was working with Christian Arabs in Akko. He was trying to get Mustafa to make a wrought iron double bed for a couple. It is customary for young couples to receive a double bed as a wedding gift, prior to getting married. Because the job required persistence and more time than most projects, Mustafa agreed very reluctantly, only because it facilitated a marriage and therefore, was considered a blessing.

Our newfound acquaintance with Earl McCoy turned out to be very interesting. A slight young man in his early 30s, of medium height, with short brownish sandy hair and blue eyes, he exuded warmth and friendliness. His partner, Reva, taught art in old Akko. The art consisted of geometric patterns or scrolls, completely non-figurative. When Reva instructed her students to "draw what you see," Earl recounted, even the very young children promptly drew abstract designs. Such was the pervasive influence of the commandment, "Thou shalt not make any graven image or likeness."

Although Earl's mandate was to work with the Christian-Arab community, he was respected and well liked by all. Since they couldn't pronounce his name, they called him "Oyl" or "McCoy." The mosque controlled much of Akko's finances, schooling, welfare, and work projects. Some of the money came from donations to the mosque and some was given to the mosque by the Israeli government. For example, for education, the amount of money given was generally half of what the Israeli government spent on Jewish schools. As a service provider to the Christian-Arab community, Earl also maintained a close and cordial relationship with the mosque. Earl's friendship provided a new perspective on the inner workings of old Akko.

Late one afternoon, Norman and I were listening to the BBC news and were shocked to hear about riots in Wadi Salib, a very poor area of Haifa near the harbour. The street demonstrations and acts of vandalism had been sparked by the wrongful shooting of a Moroccan Jewish immigrant by police officers. Demonstrators accused the police of ethnic discrimination against *Mizrahi* Jews (Jews from Arab countries).

Moroccan Jewish immigrants had been placed in the abandoned Arab houses in the Wadi Salib area by the government. The neighbourhood quickly became a neglected, over-populated slum and the Moroccans were living in poor, cramped conditions. At the same time, the Israeli government was granting newer, more spacious housing to the new Polish immigrants. This obvious discrimination against the *Mizrahim* (Easterners) was one of the main catalysts for the riots. This event highlighted the existing governmental discrimination against certain ethnic Israeli Jews.

Discovering this kind of discrimination among Jews made me sick to my stomach. I was totally disgusted. Norman tried to comfort me by saying, "Gloria, it's human nature. You just expect too much from Jews. They're like anyone else, some good, some bad."

"But we have been oppressed and discriminated against. We know how that feels. How can we do it to our own people!"

"I don't know how to answer that. It truly is a conundrum, and logically hard to understand. People don't live by logic. Enough of all this. Let's turn off the radio, get our meal from the cafeteria, and play with our wonderful kids. That's the best antidote of all."

By then, we had been in Akko nearly five months. It was now early March and flowers were abundant everywhere. Purim had come and gone. Except for a costume parade in the *gan* for the children and a parade through the main street in Akko, little note was made of the festival in the town. Akko consisted of several disparate groups and there was little community spirit there. I recalled dressing David and Tamar in their

Purim costumes on Kfar Daniel. Tamar had been dressed as an angel with an aluminum foil halo, wings and a white dress. David had been Satan, with a pitchfork and horns sprouting from his head. We were all so excited. How I missed the sweet, heartfelt community celebrations of Kfar Daniel.

I asked myself once more, *Why had I come to this country?* I had a dream. I loved the heat, the sun, the enormous sparkling stars, the brown hills waiting to be planted, the warmth and even the loud fractiousness of its people, the genuine excitement and pride in new economic development, and especially the harshness of the nuanced Hebrew language with its overlaid mystical meanings. But mostly it was my connection to Jewish history, and my link to my people. It was home. Lately, I had begun to doubt, to question; too many things were challenging my values. I felt uneasy. I sensed that Norman was also restless.

"The rumour is that there will probably be a *giyus* (call-up) sometime soon," Norman informed me. "There have been quite a few border incidents."

"Oh, Norm, will you have to go?"

"I don't know. We'll just have to wait and see."

Sure enough, three days later, every radio station was blaring out codes of soldiers' numbers and all of Israel was listening intently to their radios to hear if they would be called up. All day long it droned on and on: "Number so-and-so report to camp somewhere ... Number so-and-so report to camp somewhere else." I thought I would go mad from anxiety. Finally, it stopped. I heaved a sigh of relief. Fortunately, Norman's number was not called. Nevertheless, the tension in the country was palpable. The incursions in the South by *fellaheen*, wandering Egyptian peasants, were stopped, and the *kibbutzim* there were made more secure. Another reminder of what it was like to live in a country not at peace and always on the edge. What a country. We were as one, determined to defend our tiny nation.

I enjoyed my work, which I kept separate from my family. It belonged only to me. Norman did the same with his work. Our common language, our link, revolved around the children. I missed the socializing at Kfar Daniel, and the sharing of our work experience and personalities. Had we become two solitudes now?

Finally, I said to Norman, "We have to talk. This is no good. I feel terrible because we seem to be so unable to share. Please, speak to me. Don't shut me out. Please, Norm."

Norman quickly put his arms around me. "Gloria, I'm such a loner. I've always been a loner. I'm so sorry to shut you out. I don't mean to do it or to hurt you. I guess I just automatically go that way without even realizing the impact on you. I've just had a lot of figuring out to do. And I still don't know which way to go."

"What are you talking about, Norm?"

"I'm trying to figure out why I want to live in this country and how that will impact you and the kids."

"Don't you think you might ask me how I feel about all this?"

"Yes, but I know how you feel."

"Is that right! And how do you know?" I asked indignantly and began shouting. "Do you ever ask me? Do you talk to me about it? Or do you just assume because you are such a superior person that you know everything about me without ever needing to connect with me. What arrogance!" All my pent-up anxiety, frustration and loneliness boiled over. Tears silently streamed down my face.

Norman looked at me in astonishment, baffled by the intensity of my outburst. He hadn't been aware of how deeply hurt I was. Clearly, he needed to connect with me more deeply on a more on-going basis. But that was hard for him and he was at a loss about how to do that. He held me in his arms and kissed me. "*Chabeebi*, you mean the world to me. Don't cry, *Chabeebi*. I'm thinking that the idealism I once knew in this country is gone. It's ordinary daily life like it is in every country. If I have to chase the lira six days a week, I'd rather chase the buck in Canada five days a week."

"You want to go home, back to Canada?" I asked incredulously.

"I'm not sure. But I think so. You want to stay, don't you?"

"I don't know anymore. I feel this is my country. But I don't feel as comfortable here as I did before. I worry if this country will be good for our kids. I keep thinking about what Darwin said about the education system. And, although my Hebrew is getting better all the time, I'll never be as fluent in Hebrew as I am in English. I remember how I felt as a first-generation child with immigrant parents and I don't want our children to feel that way about us. I don't know, Norm. I have such conflicted feelings."

"Well, for right this moment, I think we should go to bed and make love. A decision will find its own way and will become clear to us when we are ready."

CHAPTER 11

Kissing an Old Dream Goodbye

All the world is a very narrow bridge,
But the main thing is to have no fear at all.
— Rabbi Nachman of Bratislava

I began making lists, pro and con. I put down everything, from highly valued concerns down to the most trivial. On one side, I wrote all the reasons for staying in Israel. On the other, I stated all my doubts — certain negative societal attitudes, my children's potential educational system, political injustices, corruption in the form of "*protexia*," and the top-heavy inflexible bureaucracy.

Amazed, I looked again and again; the lists seemed almost equally balanced. I became profoundly conflicted and troubled. All my life, living in Israel had been my dream. If not this, what was my dream? What about my family? What about Norman, my husband? To give up my dream felt like a betrayal of my values, my people. What to do? What to do?

We continued our daily routines. I went to my job and picked up the children from the *gan*. Norman arrived home in the early afternoon. Most of our evenings were spent with Mustafa and Subhia. Somehow, the spirit had gone out of all our efforts. Finally, at the end of June, Norman turned to me and said, "I think I need to apply for an exit permit from the army. What do you think, Gloria?"

"Are you asking me whether I've made a decision to leave Israel, Norm?"

"I guess, in my roundabout way, I am. My heart just isn't in it anymore."

"I know. We can't live here like this. That's for sure. I'm with you, Norm. Somehow, I feel terrible. I feel like such a failure, to be going back to Canada. It's just hard to give up on my dream." Norman put his arms around me and tried to comfort me. "So what do we do now?"

"I'll write to the Commanding Officer of my unit and request an exit permit from the army."

A week later, Norman received a letter from the Jewish Agency citing the contract that Norman and I had signed: that the *Sochnut* would loan us the fare to immigrate to Israel, which would be forgiven provided we remained in the country for a minimum of two years. Since we had been in Israel for only 22 months, we would have to pay back the entire fare, $3,500, before Norman could get an exit permit from the army. We were in shock! We looked at each other, totally baffled.

"Do you remember ever signing such an arrangement?"

"No, do you?"

"No. I remember them saying that the *Sochnut* would pay for everything for us because we were *Olim Chadashim* (new immigrants). What shall we do, Norm? I don't want to return to Canada with a huge debt."

"I have an army friend, Tsvi Rimmer. He is now a captain and head of the tank school. I'll give him a call." Three hours later, Norman filled me in. "This is unbelievable. Tsvi had no idea. It seems the process of getting an army exit permit has gotten tighter and tighter over the years. He will do whatever he can but he doesn't hold out much hope. He said the bureaucracy at the *Sochnut* is the very worst of all the bureaucracies in Israel, the oldest and the most entrenched."

Dispirited, we carried on. "I think Yishai and Mahrie in Kfar Daniel may be in the same boat as us," I told Norman one day. "They can hardly wait to get back to Manchester. I'll give them a call and see if they have had any luck in getting Yishai's army exit permit." When I got off the phone with Mahrie, I was fuming. "I can't believe this. They were so intimidated by that goddam *Sochnut* that Yishai's brother in Manchester got a loan to pay the *Sochnut* to get Yishai's exit permit. This is insane."

"We may have to do something like that or just stay two more months and be done with them," said Norman.

"This is pure Israeli bureaucracy wielding its mighty power. Let me think about this. There must be a way.

This is all a game of bluff. Their bluff of power certainly is intimidating." I paused. "Unless ... I can out-bluff them? I still love Israel, but I detest the worst bureaucracy in Israel, the Jewish Agency."

Three days later, I sat down and composed the following letter to Senator Auchincloss, the representative from New Jersey.

> Dear Sir,
>
> I am one of your constituents in New Jersey and holder of U.S. passport # GB 215503. The Zionist organization is holding me and my family here in Israel hostage against our will. We agreed to come to Israel in September 1957. Feeling very favorably disposed toward Israel, we entered an agreement in good faith. Now that we wish to return to the United States, they are holding us for ransom and wish a payment of $3,500, which we frankly do not have. This is unconscionable! However, I think the State Department should take a second look at their policy vis-à-vis Israel and its Zionist activity within the United States. They deceive young idealistic American families into leaving their native land to live in a foreign state without openly showing their nefarious intentions. This is scandalous. They really should be investigated. Please help this American in distress.
>
> Thank you.
>
> Sincerely,
> Gloria Levi née Hammerman
> cc. Jewish Agency of Israel

I sent the copy of the letter to the *Sochnut,* without ever sending the original letter to Senator Auchincloss.

Three days later, Norman received his army exit permit. I was triumphant. I had out-bluffed the star bluffer!

Life became hectic. What to tell the children? How to tell the children? They had been uprooted twice before. This would be their third loss of friends and familiar surroundings. I felt so guilty. Norman tried to save the day. He sat down with David and Tamar. "We are going to go on a big adventure. We will go to England and you will be able to meet a bunch of new cousins, just like you, and aunts and uncles. Then, we'll finally go home, back to Canada ... to our own house there. So, we won't have to move around to new places all the time. Would you like that?"

"Yes, but what about Ephraim and Amichai and my friends here, Yoni and Moti? I have to see them too," David said.

Stumped, Norman gave David a big hug. "I'm really sorry, David. I know how much you like your friends. Perhaps, in the meantime, I could be an extra special friend to play with as well as being your Dad. Would you like that?"

"Yeh, let's play scouts and enemies. I'm a scout and you are the enemy. Are you going to hide?"

"Let's save it for another time, okay?" As Norman left the room, he quietly said to me, "I see what you mean. I feel terrible."

Tamar became quieter and more clingy. I held her, hugged her and kissed her a lot. I recognized the role we had all played indirectly in increasing Tamar's timidity.

Soon it was July, a busy time of sorting out our income, paying bills and debts. Since paydays had never been regularized through the bureaucracy, some payments were loans, while others were compensation for labour. It was a convoluted Israeli system. Clarifying our finances was complicated. Getting rid of household effects took time and effort. The most difficult moments were telling friends and relatives that we were leaving. How could we admit to our cousins Mordechai and Chana in Balfouria that we were leaving? Mordechai and Chana had also immigrated from America. But they had done it in 1923 and had come to Palestine with eight very young daughters. Their stories had always inspired me. Now, while visiting them, I felt ashamed of our decision. It was painful indeed.

The farewell visit to Kfar Daniel was a mixture of loving embraces, tears, and assurances of staying in touch. When David said goodbye to Amichai and Ephraim, I nearly broke down. David put his arm around Amichai and said, "I don't want to go, Amichai, but my *Abba* says I have to. Maybe you can come and see me? I'll share my toys with you. My *Ima* will help me write a letter to you with our new address. Bye." Then he shouted loudly, "C'mon, *Ima*, let's go!"

On our final night in Akko, Norman, David, Tamar and I solemnly walked into the old city to Mustafa's house, each pushing a suitcase. Dinner was waiting for us. We sat down and slowly, silently began to eat. Sadness permeated the air. After dinner, Subhia showed me where we would sleep and helped me get David and Tamar ready for bed. Mustafa beckoned to Norman to follow him to another room. There, Mustafa took out a large wad of American hundred-dollar bills. "I will go down with you to the *namal* (port), and if for some reason they try to hold you up for the money the *Sochnut* says you owe, I will pay them the money they are asking for."

Norman was struck dumb. "You are truly a brother. I shall never forget this." They hugged each other with deep affection.

Fortunately, the exit process went smoothly. There was no need for Mustafa's money. My last memory is of standing on the deck of the ship, looking down at Mustafa waving with tears streaming down his face, as we pulled away from shore. The ship's horn blasted as we got underway. The four of us turned, and with heart-breaking sadness, silently walked toward our cabin.

Moments in Time — Musings

1964

I looked out of the windows of my modern post-and-beam home in Deep Cove. It was a typical wet Vancouver spring. Our back garden was a lush emerald green, a cherished colour. A constant gentle rain had been falling for two days. The green leaves of the trees were dripping from the rain. Green. Everything was green.

Today was Shavuot, the time of receiving the Ten Commandments, our foundational moral compass. Shavuot, a harvest holiday, celebrating spring. I looked at David and Tamar, now 10 and 9, watching TV. I thought back to another Shavuot in Israel, five years earlier. Our children, with garlands of flowers in their hair, dressed all in white, had proudly marched to the makeshift stage in the field carrying their sprouted plants. Whatever happened to my dream of proud confident Hebrew-speaking youth living within a Jewish calendar of time, infusing ancient traditions with new meaning and vitality? It was another world ... another time.

I had been there in 1950, two years after the State of Israel was born. Those had been heady times. I had watched as two old Moroccan Jewish men walked down the gangplank of a ship, each carrying a Torah scroll, bending, and kissing the soil of the Holy Land of Israel. It was so dramatic. Some had come seeking refuge, with little more than the clothes they were wearing, traumatized by the horrors of World War II. Some walked down the gangplank reciting verses from the Bible. It was an inspiring time.

They came to a land devoid of most natural resources. Except for the Jezreel Valley in the North, it was a barren, brown, treeless land of rocks and stones. By sheer grit and determination, they forged an economy. Multiple *kibbutzim* expanded and dotted the countryside. Tens of thousands of Holocaust survivors poured into the nascent state, healing and dedicating their lives to creating a just and compassionate state. Effective national institutions were established. Resources and industries were developed. Construction was everywhere. Towns, villages and cities appeared. Culture flourished. Pride and excitement were palpable. A state was being formed. My people, my heritage, my history, my language, my customs and values. I loved and identified with it all.

The early founders were ideologues, driven by a dream of building a new society, socially just and equitable. Driven by a sense of self-righteousness, they were harsh, rigid, but also inspiring leaders. I discovered years later that, in 1948, the Israeli leadership had expelled the entire Arab population of Lod from their homes, thereby providing a freer, safer place for new Jewish immigrants. We were building a state. As one granddaughter challenged me, "Was one group's blood more precious than the other's?" In their zeal to build a new society, the Arabs, "the others" in the land, did not even register on their radar. The Arabs were merely a part of the landscape, like a tree or a stream, without feelings, relationships, hurts or dreams. Except for a few brave, knowledgeable people, those ideologues did not recognize them as fellow human beings. They neither saw nor heard them, except as an existential threat. With such unawareness, they were able to blindly continue to inflict pain on "the other."

1967

Egypt, Syria and Jordan, with their superior manpower and weapons, planned to attack Israel from three sides. Memories of the Holocaust were too recent and stirred terror in the hearts of Israelis. Israel launched a pre-emptive strike, defeating the opposing forces in six days!

After the 1967 Six Day War, a sense of triumphalism developed. With their historical sensitivity to existential danger, Israelis also developed an increased sense of superiority and smug self-righteousness. Thus, they were able to suspend their inherent ethical traditions and inflict pain on "the other." They occupied populated Palestinian land and oppressed their hostile neighbours. Cynical and corrupt, more recent Israeli governments have repeatedly paid lip service to peace statements while continuing to appropriate Arab land. Nationalist Orthodox Jews have been the worst oppressors, justifying their behaviour in the name of God. Using God's name to justify evil is truly a desecration, *Chilul HaShem.*

The Bible says over and over again, "You shall love the stranger who dwells amongst you, for you were strangers in the Land of Egypt." As long as Israelis feel an existential threat, this commandment will be cast aside. How can a group wielding excessive power over a much weaker opponent still see itself as the victim? Can so many years of persecution and affliction create an almost permanent scar of 'victim'?

As long as each group is consumed with its own pain, they are unable to comprehend or feel the pain of the other. I fear for my beloved country on its present suicidal course. I weep for the loss of my dream of a righteous people trying to live a life of social justice, compassion and harmony.

As Ari Shavit wrote in *The Promised Land*: "Erased from memory is the land that was, the diaspora that was, the injustice done to them and the genocide done to us." With tears in my eyes, I kissed an old dream goodbye.

Fast forward to 2019

I am an old woman now, with middle-aged children, adult grandchildren and young great grandchildren. After 32 years of marriage, Norman and I separated in 1983. It was a time of great personal upheaval, moving from years of being a couple to singleness, to experiencing the bitterness of unrequited love, to re-evaluating everything I held near and dear. I learned and grew in strength, resilience and self-acceptance. Deep reciprocal affection between my children and me sustains me. My grandchildren continue to be a delight and a joy. An extensive network of friends stimulates and supports me.

I joined an egalitarian Renewal synagogue. I have been studying Jewish texts for some 18 years, spending summers at women's *yeshivahs* in Jerusalem. My political and social activism continues. I have become more engaged in Jewish mysticism and the wisdom texts. I have discovered the power of meditation and the richness of Buddha's teachings. My life today is full of love, joy and wonder. I feel truly blessed to have lived in Canada most of my life and fully appreciate Canada's extraordinary physical beauty, its moderation and tolerance, and its general kindness.

Never before in Jewish history have Jews lived in such a free society with so much genuine opportunity and ability to intermingle and participate freely. However, this freedom of opportunity has also led to extensive assimilation. As with other ancient cultures, will the unique, particularistic Jewish voice of the universal be lost forever?

Two of my children have married non-Jewish partners. Of my seven partnered grandchildren, five live with non-Jewish partners. Will I be the last link in the chain of my Jewish history?

I am a link in a 3,000-year history, and I feel a dread that that link with history will be broken, either by my children or possibly by my grandchildren. I feel an imperative to preserve and transmit my Jewish heritage. How? It is an uphill battle in North America. In this age of nuclear families, can I ever really convey the sense of security, liveliness and warmth of extended family, the sense of support and safety gleaned from the community that I knew in my childhood. The richness of lifecycle celebrations, the awareness of our history, the writings of our sages, and the desire to turn and return again and again to our foundational sources.

I see a trend of sameness. I fear there will be an extinction of differences into a bland homogenization of mass culture. I prefer to see myself as an individual player in an orchestra, where together the beautiful notes of each cherished instrument contribute to the glorious sound of a symphony. How do you make that happen? It's a puzzle. I comfort myself by admitting that I don't know. All I can do is to try to transmit my knowledge, love, and caring for Judaism to my children, to the next generation, recognizing that it is an uphill battle. Perhaps, in contrast to the extreme, fundamentalist ultra-

Orthodox, a small new vital remnant will grow through Jewish Renewal.

I feel a heavy responsibility to play my role. What is my role? What is my responsibility to my history? To my tribe? To "the other"? Who is "the other"? For centuries, Jews have been seen as "the other." We know how it feels to be ostracized, on the outside, unrecognized and discounted. As I look out from the warmth of my community, my tribe, I see the non-Jew as "the other." However, by turning inward, we have become ethnocentric and xenophobic.

We need a new paradigm, one that mutually honours and celebrates the love and beauty in each other's traditions and practices. I have learned that immersing myself in the ritualistic and spiritual beauty of the other's traditions and customs does not make me less Jewish. I have learned that it can only enrich me. We need to build a world in which we are not afraid of "the other" and recognize that the other, the stranger, the *ger b'tochem* with whom we live, is our brother and sister. We need to welcome and honour the other, make room for the other, and build a world that celebrates our diversity; that says that "otherness" is beautiful. *Ken yihee ratson.* May it be so.

ABOUT THE AUTHOR

Speaker, activist and author, Gloria Levi was born and raised in New York City, and has lived in Israel and Canada. A gerontologist with more than 30 years' experience in the field, Gloria has worked as a recreation therapist, social worker, trainer/consultant in aging, and a community volunteer coordinator. Her series of six booklets, *Challenges of Later Life* (1992) was widely distributed throughout Canada. Her book, *Dealing With Memory Changes As You Grow Older* (Bantam, 1998), co-authored with Kathleen Gose, has been translated into six languages.

A political activist, Gloria served as a councillor on Coquitlam Council from 1981 to 1984. She later established Habitat for Humanity of Greater Vancouver and helped build 27 houses, from 1997 to 2004.

A dedicated student of Judaic studies, she translated the story of a Chasidic master, *The Life and Times of Simcha Bunim of P'shischa* (2007), from the original Hebrew.

Gloria published her first memoir, *My Dance with Shechina*, in 2012, followed by her second memoir, *Kissing an Old Dream Goodbye* (Fictive Press), in 2019. A mother of five, a grandmother of 11 and a great grandmother of seven, she lives in Vancouver, British Columbia.

ACKNOWLEDGEMENTS

I started to write with a small idea to simply describe some of the minutiae of communal life. I would like to thank my writer friend, Charlotte Cameron, whose curiosity kept prompting me to amplify my story. I was fortunate to have Bonnie Sher Klein and Rhea Page as readers whose supportive comments and critical eyes helped shaped the book. I owe Barbara Pulling, an editor par excellence, a debt of gratitude who affirmed my unique voice and my writing when I needed it most. Finally, I want to thank my family who inspire me and are always there for me. All of you are always there for each other, and me, fun-loving, caring, and vibrant.